EPIC CARDBOARD ADVENTURES

BY

LESLIE MANLAPIG

Capstone Young Readers
a capstone imprint

TABLE OF

CONTENTS

Have you dreamed of traveling the world? Going back in time? Putting on a show? This book will help you do all that and more, using . . .

CARDBOARD!

⊱ Yes, that's right! ⊰

The boxes sitting around your house can be used to make your very own adventures. All you need are some simple supplies, a willing adult helper, and an awesome imagination!

Haven't built anything before? Don't worry! The STEP-BY-STEP instructions will walk you through all the projects, and before you know it, you'll be sitting in your very own spaceship wearing snowshoes and accepting an Academy Award!

CLAP
CLAP
CLAP

SUPPLIES

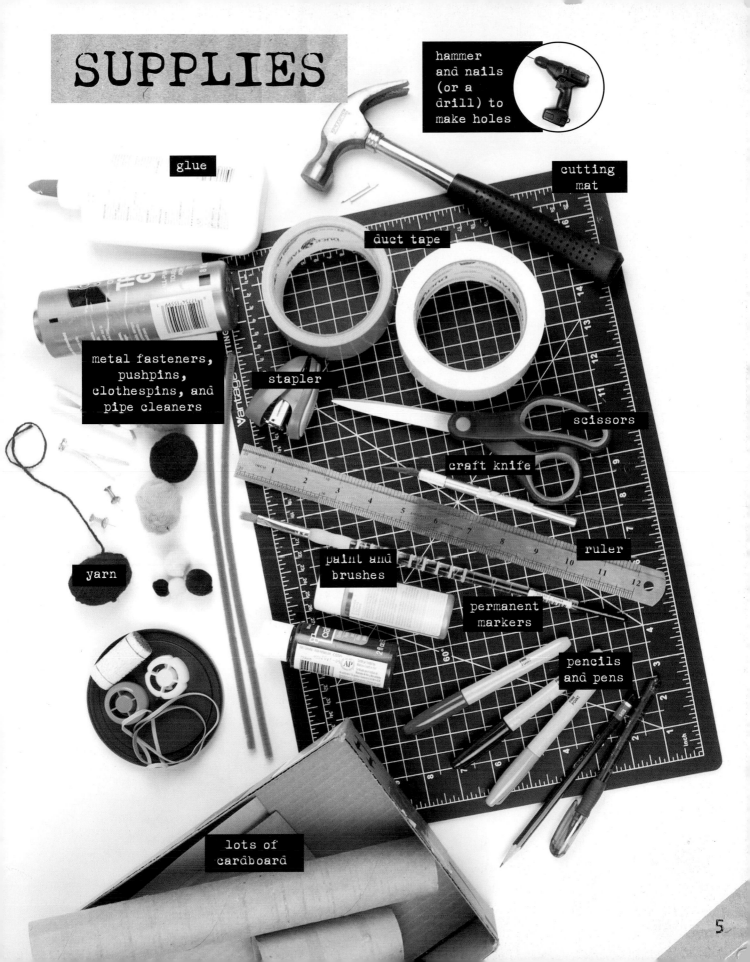

hammer and nails (or a drill) to make holes

glue

cutting mat

duct tape

metal fasteners, pushpins, clothespins, and pipe cleaners

stapler

scissors

craft knife

ruler

yarn

paint and brushes

permanent markers

pencils and pens

lots of cardboard

EXPLORE

Arctic
Explorer

Jungle Explorer

Deep Sea

THE WORLD

Ancient Egypt

PROJECT #1
SPACE SHUTTLE

Ever wonder how a space shuttle blasts off into space? Powerful rocket boosters and an external fuel tank thrust the space shuttle into orbit. Once they are no longer needed. The rocket boosters and fuel tank detach from the shuttle. Recreate this amazing launch sequence with this easy-to-build cardboard toy!

SUPPLIES

- scissors
- 1 paper towel roll
- cardboard (use thin, non-corrugated cereal box cardboard)

- 1 toilet paper roll
- white and red paint
- paintbrush
- black and orange permanent markers

- orange and white duct tape
- hot glue gun
- hook and loop fastener (optional)

1 Cut your paper towel roll into two unequal rolls.

The longer roll will be your fuel tank.

The shorter roll will be your space shuttle.

2 (For space shuttle)
Cut out a tail piece from the cereal box. Cut one slit on each side so it attaches to your cardboard roll. Cut out matching slits into your paper towel roll.

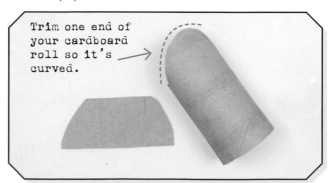

Trim one end of your cardboard roll so it's curved.

(For external fuel tank)

Trim one end of your cardboard roll so it's curved (similar to the space shuttle).

 (For rocket boosters)

Cut your toilet roll tube in half lengthwise. Trim one end of each so they're curved.

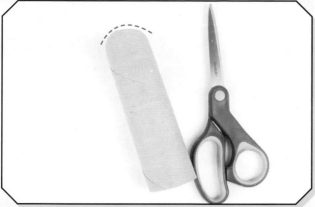

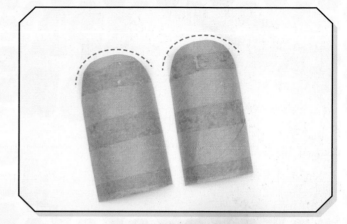

 Paint your space shuttle (white), external fuel tank (red), and rocket boosters (white). Use permanent markers or duct tape to add extra detail. Roll up your rockets and use duct tape to secure them.

 Hot glue your rockets, space shuttle, and fuel tank together.

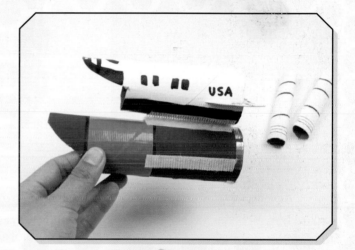

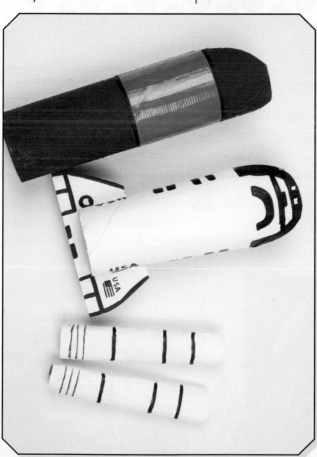

TIP

1. You can use white glue instead of a hot glue gun, though it will take longer to dry.

2. Use the hook and loop fastener to give this project a more realistic touch!

PROJECT #2
SPACESHIP CONTROLS

It's 20 years in the future. You're an astronaut ready to take your first flight. Where would you fly? What would the inside of your spaceship look like? It's time to build your dream ride!

SUPPLIES

- cardboard box
- duct tape
- various everyday items: bottle caps, egg cartons, calculators, stickers, black paper, clothespins, magnets, metal lids, golf tees, CDs, plastic lids, buttons, old electronic equipment, plastic bottles, rubber bands, skewers
- cutting mat
- scissors
- black paper
- white pencil
- glue (hot glue or tacky glue)
- drill (or hammer and nail)

1 Find a clean cardboard box and decorate with paint or duct tape.

2 Look for an assortment of items to use as buttons, dials, screens, and switches.

SEARCH TIP: Look in the recycling bin or use old electronic equipment!

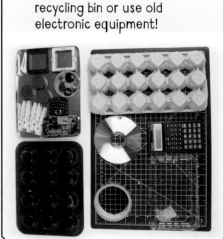

3 **(To create screens)**
Cut out rectangles and squares from black paper. Use a white pencil to draw on details.

 4 Use hot glue, tacky glue, or duct tape to adhere your console.

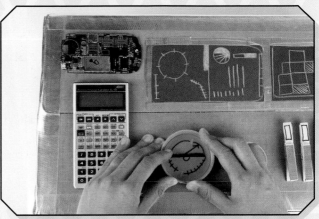

 5 **(To create a joystick)**

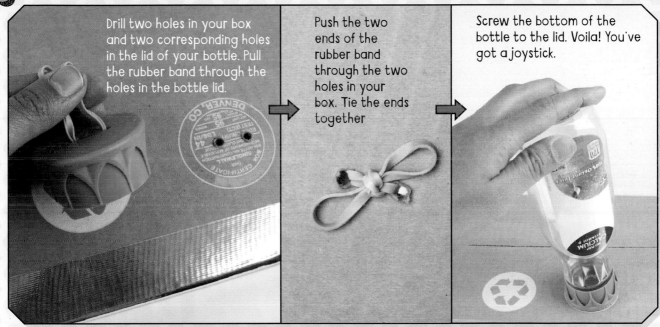

Drill two holes in your box and two corresponding holes in the lid of your bottle. Pull the rubber band through the holes in the bottle lid.

Push the two ends of the rubber band through the two holes in your box. Tie the ends together

Screw the bottom of the bottle to the lid. Voila! You've got a joystick.

TIP

1. Use a skewer to push the rubber band through the holes in the bottle lid.

2. Decorate your console with a permanent marker and duct tape!

3. Ask your adult helper to drill or hammer.

PROJECT #3

SPACE HELMET

You've finally blasted into outer space. Congratulations! Are you ready to explore the great beyond? This helmet will help you take one giant leap for humankind!

SUPPLIES

- scissors
- paper grocery bag
- black paint
- paintbrush
- white paper
- drawing supplies (white and other colored pencils, permanent markers, pens)
- white and silver duct tape
- cutting mat
- craft knife
- plastic container
- corrugated cardboard
- hot glue

1 Trim your paper grocery bag so it fits nicely on your head. Paint it black.

2 Sketch and cut out a design for a helmet.

Keep in mind where you want to put your visor.

3 Tape similarly sized strips of duct tape onto a cutting mat. Make sure they overlap to create a duct tape sheet.

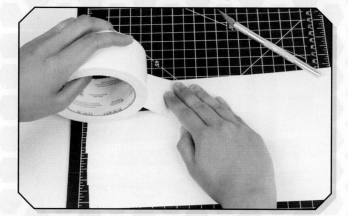

 4 Place your helmet on top of the duct tape sheet. Trace it and use your craft knife to cut out the helmet.

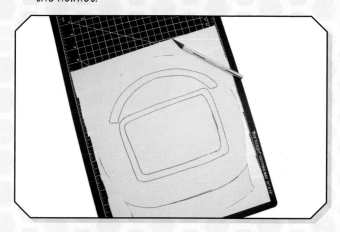

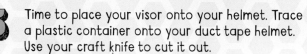 **5** Time to place your visor onto your helmet. Trace a plastic container onto your duct tape helmet. Use your craft knife to cut it out.

 6 Stick your duct tape helmet onto your painted paper bag.

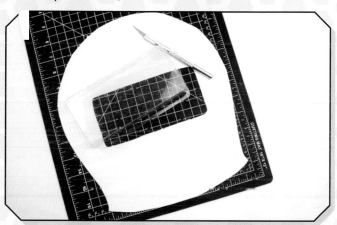

7

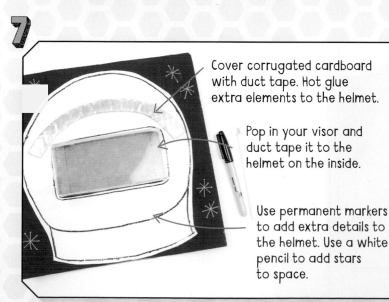

Cover corrugated cardboard with duct tape. Hot glue extra elements to the helmet.

Pop in your visor and duct tape it to the helmet on the inside.

Use permanent markers to add extra details to the helmet. Use a white pencil to add stars to space.

PROJECT #1

SCUBA MASK

There are many beautiful and mysterious sea animals. Take a closer look at them with this scuba mask. Happy swimming!

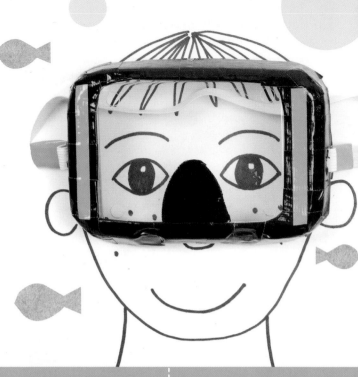

- plastic berry lid
- scissors
- cutting mat
- egg carton
- pencil
- craft knife
- black and green duct tape
- elastic
- stapler

1 Clean your plastic berry lid and let it dry. Cut the lid so it's nice and flat.

2 Cut the lid off of your egg carton. Trace the lid onto the egg carton and cut that portion out with a craft knife. Continue to shape the egg carton into a scuba mask shape. Trim it so it's just a little flatter.

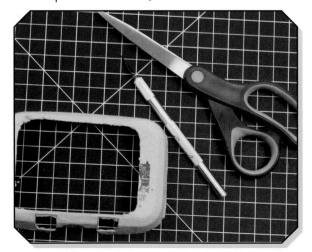

Cut out a section on the bottom edge of the egg carton for your nose.

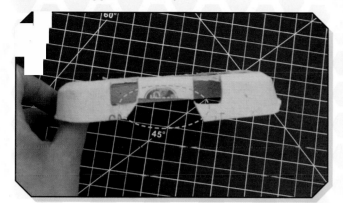

 Cut out one slit on each side of the egg carton for the strap.

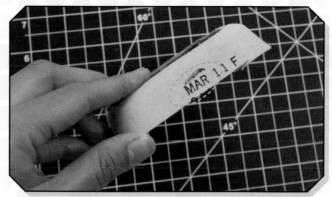

 Cut strips of duct tape and use them to decorate the egg carton. Additionally, use duct tape to stick your plastic lid on.

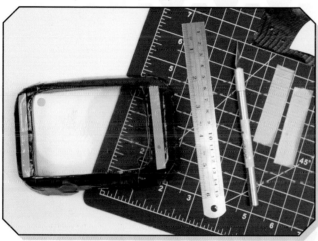

To make the strap, slide a strip of elastic through the side slits and staple them together.

Cover up the staples with duct tape.

DON'T HAVE ELASTIC?

TRY THESE INSTEAD!

Yarn

String

Or make a strap using duct tape and Velcro

PROJECT #2

BOAT DESIGN

Ready to sail the seven seas? Design and create your very own cardboard boats. You can even test them out on the water!

SUPPLIES

- paper
- pencil
- ruler
- cardboard
- scissors
- craft knife
- cutting mat
- duct tape
- permanent markers
- large container of water (or bathtub or pool)

1 Draw one or more of these designs onto paper to use as templates. Solid lines note where you will cut the cardboard. Dotted lines note where you will score and bend the cardboard.

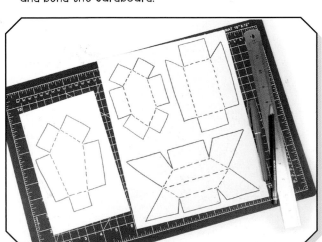

2 Trace the templates directly onto cardboard to make identically sized boats. (Or you can draw larger versions of your templates onto cardboard.) Cut out.

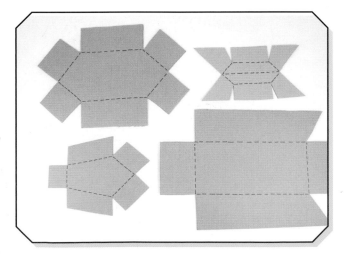

Score the dotted lines with a craft knife (run the knife over the cardboard). Make sure you don't cut completely through the cardboard!

You are just cutting the top layer of cardboard so it bends easily. The cardboard still needs to be connected.

 Fold up the flaps and tape them together.

 Decorate your boat with duct tape and permanent markers.

Make sure you use permanent markers. They will not bleed in water.

 Once you're ready, put your boat in the water. Does it float? Will it carry weight? Which boat design seems to float the best?

TIP
To make your boat last longer cover it completely with duct tape.

PROJECT #3
SHARK FIN

Ahh! What's that lurking in the water? Scare friends and family by transforming yourself into one of the most frightening ocean predators – a shark!

SUPPLIES

- corrugated cardboard
- scissors
- tacky glue
- paint and paintbrush
- ruler
- duct tape
- craft knife
- cutting mat
- clear tape

1 Cut a rectangle out of cardboard. This will be your back piece. It should sit and fit between your shoulders like a backpack would.

2 Cut out two fin shapes from cardboard. They should be approximately the same length as your back piece

3 Cut out four slits, one in each corner of your back piece. They should be as wide as your duct tape. Also cut out a slit in the middle of your back piece.

TIP
You can also just cut out one fin shape if you're short on time or cardboard.

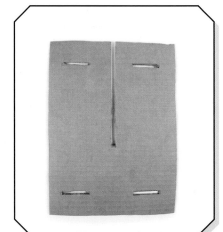

18

4 Cut out a slit in each of the fin pieces. They should be in identical locations.

 5 Use tacky glue to glue your fin pieces together.

 6 Paint your fin and back piece.

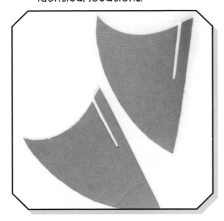

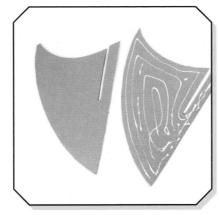

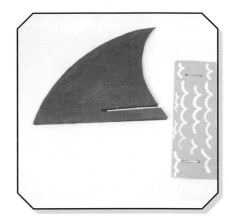

7 (To make duct tape straps)

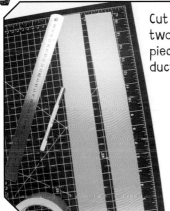

Cut out two long pieces of duct tape.

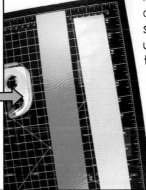

Flip one strip over so it is sticky-side up. Use clear tape to hold it in place. Place the other piece of duct tape over it. This is a strap.

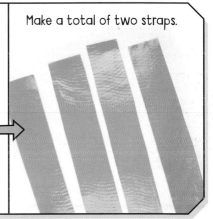

Make a total of two straps.

8 Slide the fin into the slit in the middle of the back piece. Insert a strap into the slit in one of the corners. Pull it through the slit in the opposite corner, running it the same direction as the fin.

9 Use a piece of duct tape to tape the ends of your straps together. Slip the srtaps over your shoulders and you are a shark!

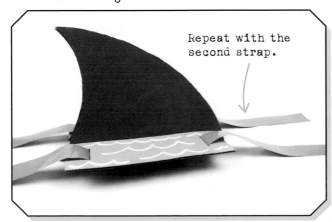

Repeat with the second strap.

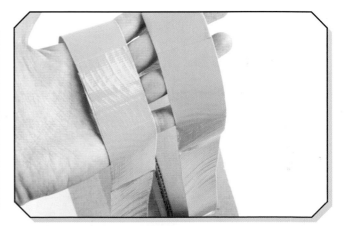

19

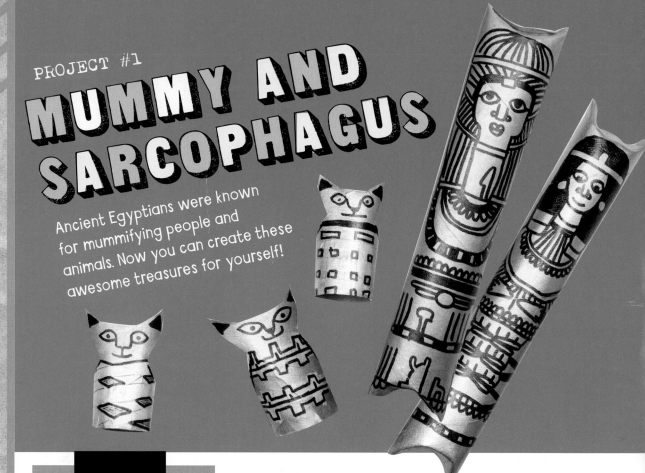

PROJECT #1

MUMMY AND SARCOPHAGUS

Ancient Egyptians were known for mummifying people and animals. Now you can create these awesome treasures for yourself!

SUPPLIES

- corrugated cardboard
- scissors
- black paint
- paintbrush
- white pencil
- masking tape
- paper towel rolls
- toilet paper rolls
- various shades of gold paint
- permanent marker

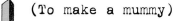

(To make a mummy)

Cut the corrugated cardboard into a mummy shape. Paint the mummy black.

Use a white pencil to draw a face, hands, and feet. Then use masking tape to "wrap" your mummy.

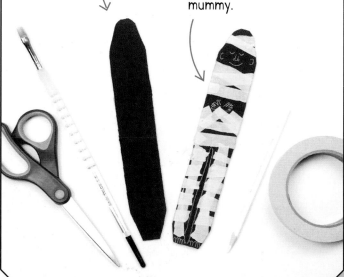

2 Push down on both sides of the paper towel roll to close the ends of the sarcophagus.

 3 Add details with a marker. You can then add your mummy and close it up in your sarcophagus!

Paint your sarcophagus gold.

(To make mummy cats)

 4 Cut out a cat shape in the front of a toilet paper roll.

 5 Place pieces of masking tape in different directions on your cat mummy.

Trim the back so it's flat.

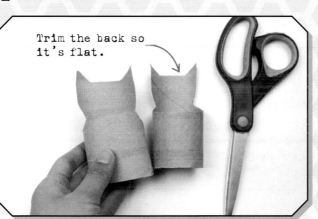

 6 Paint and use marker to add details.

PROJECT #2

PYRAMID

The ancient pyramids of Egypt are one of the most amazing wonders of the world. Ready to make one for yourself?

SUPPLIES

- large corrugated cardboard boxes
- scissors
- pencil
- duct tape
- craft paint
- paintbrush
- permanent marker

 Cut out three large isosceles triangles from your large cardboard boxes. An isosceles triangle has two sides that are the same length.

The triangles should be taller than your seated height.

TIP
No large boxes? Duct tape several cardboard sheets together to make a large enough pyramid.

Take one large triangle and trace the top portion onto a piece of cardboard. Then cut out this smaller triangle.

This will be the front of your pyramid.

Use duct tape to attach all the cardboard triangles.

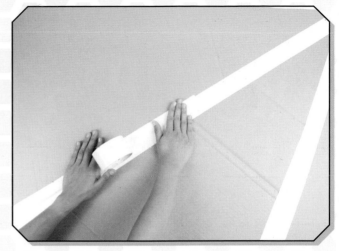

4 Make sure to duct tape the pieces together on both the inside and outside of your pyramid.

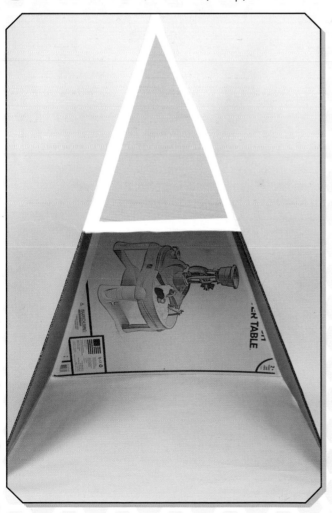

5 Decorate your pyramid with paint and permanent marker.

PROJECT #3

PHARAOH HEADDRESS

Want to strut your stuff like King Tut? Now's your chance with this ultra-rad headdress worthy of all the pharaohs of Egypt!

SUPPLIES

- measuring tape
- cereal box
- ruler
- scissors
- gold and black duct tape
- craft knife
- cutting mat
- stapler

Ask an adult to measure around your head. Cut two strips from a cereal box that are a bit longer than needed to go around your head.

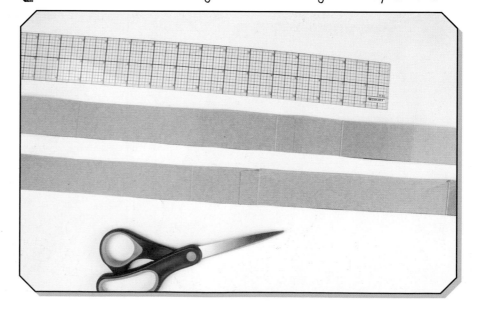

2 Cover the strips with gold duct tape.

 3 Staple the strips together so they create a frame that fits comfortably around your head.

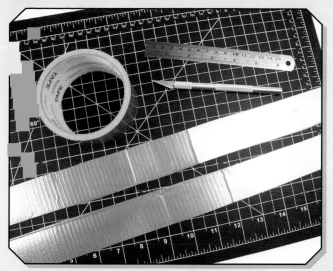

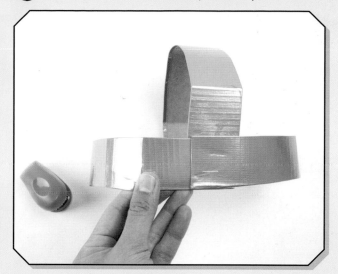

 4 Cut out a piece of cereal box into a half circle. This will be the front of your headdress. Cover it with strips of gold duct tape.

5 Cut out two identical side pieces from your cereal box. Cover them with strips of duct tape. Trim off any excess duct tape.

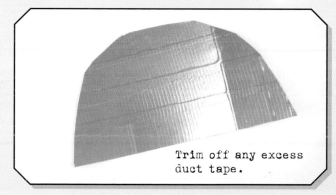

    Trim off any excess
    duct tape.

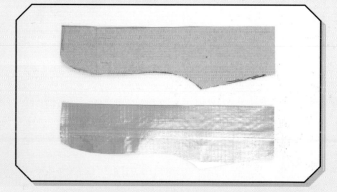

 6 Tape or staple the two side pieces on. Then cut out strips of black duct tape to decorate.

 7 Once you're finished, staple the front of the headdress onto your frame. Use a strip of gold duct tape to cover the staples.

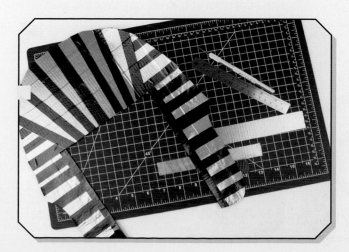

PROJECT #1

ADJUSTABLE BINOCULARS

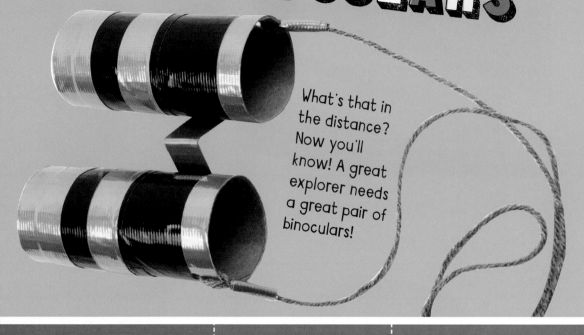

What's that in the distance? Now you'll know! A great explorer needs a great pair of binoculars!

SUPPLIES

- thin cardboard (non-corrugated)
- scissors
- 2 toilet paper rolls
- gold and black duct tape
- cutting mat
- craft knife
- stapler
- hole punch
- yarn

1 Cut out a small rectangle from thin cardboard.

about 3¼ inches x ¾ inch (8.3 centimeters x 1.9 cm)

2 Decorate your toilet paper rolls and thin cardboard rectangle with black and gold duct tape. Trim off any excess tape.

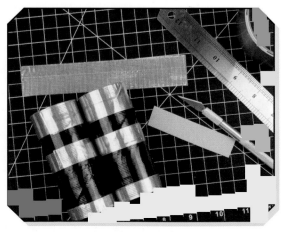

3 Staple the thin cardboard rectangle between the two toilet paper rolls.

4 Punch a hole on each side of your rolls.

5 Tie a piece of yarn (or string) through the holes in your cardboard rolls.

6 Use duct tape to cover your knots. Now you can use your binoculars to explore!

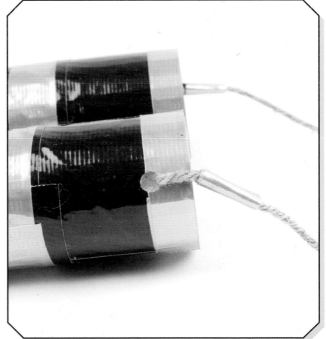

PROJECT #2

CLAWS

What's that shadow moving in the distance? A panther? A lion? Nope. It's you! Experience being the ruler of the jungle with a set of cardboard claws. Rawr!

SUPPLIES

- corrugated cardboard
- scissors
- paint and paintbrush
- pencil
- paper
- hot glue

 Cut out six cardboard claws and two cardboard hand bars. The claws should be pointed in front and curved in the back.

Design the curve so that the pieces rest comfortably against the webs of your hand.

2 Paint your claws and let them dry.

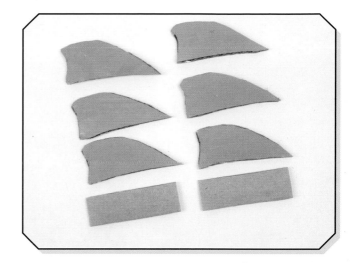

3 Hold a hand bar in your hand so one edge rests in your knuckles. Loosely wrap your fingers around it. Mark the spaces between your fingers. Do this for both hand bars.

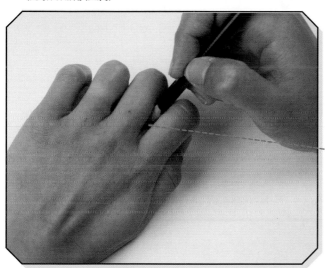

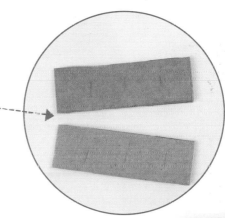

4 Hot glue a claw onto each of the markings.

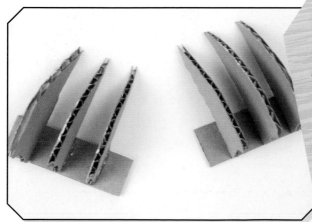

PROJECT #3

EXPLORER BAG

Ready to go on a great adventure? What will you pack? A compass? Binoculars? First aid kit? Be prepared for any adventure with this duct tape explorer's bag!

SUPPLIES

- paper
- pencil
- scissors
- brown, black, green, orange duct tape
- craft knife
- cutting mat
- trash bag

(To make a template)

Draw one square for the front of the bag and one rectangle for the back. Cut out.

Both squares should have the same width.

back

front

(To make the back piece)
Cut out strips of duct tape and stick them together, slightly overlapping each strip. Make sure it's bigger than your template's back rectangle.

 Starting from one corner, carefully peel your sheet of duct tape off the mat. Flip it over so the sticky side is up. Place a sheet of the trash bag onto the sticky side.

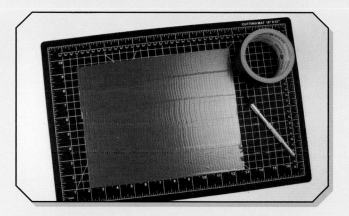

TIP

Rub the garbage bag to get rid of air bubbles and flatten wrinkles.

 Trace your template onto your sheet of duct tape. Cut it out.

 Tape the front and back pieces together. Cut out strips of duct tape to add more design details to your bag.

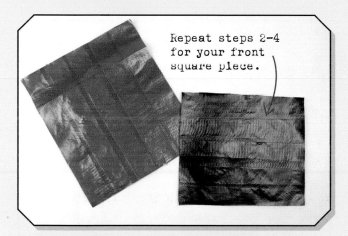

Repeat steps 2-4 for your front square piece.

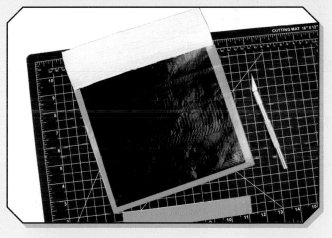

 Cut a 16-inch (41-cm) piece of duct tape. Flip it over so the sticky side is up. Fold over one side to the middle, lengthwise. Fold the other side on top of it. Now you have a strap! Tape it to the back of your bag.

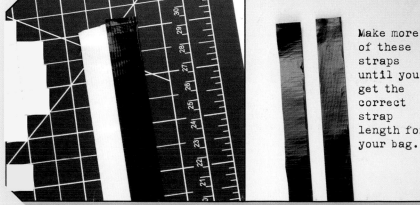

Make more of these straps until you get the correct strap length for your bag.

PROJECT #1

SLED

Every Arctic explorer needs a handy sled to carry materials and friends. Time to sail over the snow with your own creation!

SUPPLIES

- shoe box
- corrugated cardboard
- permanent marker
- scissors
- tacky glue
- paint and paintbrush
- hammer and nail
- yarn

 1 Grab a shoe box without the lid.

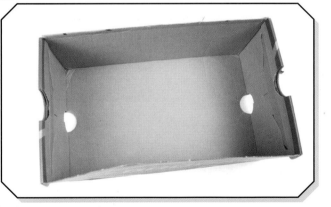

2

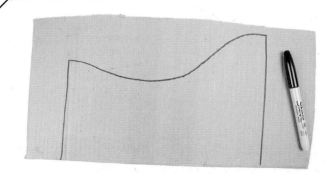

Trace two sled shapes onto a piece of cardboard.

Cut out each sled shape.

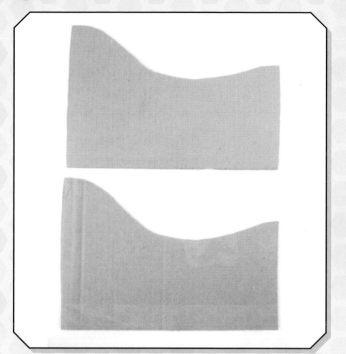

 Use tacky glue to attach the two sides of the sled onto the shoe box.

TIP
Place a book on top of the sled to keep the sides in place.

 Paint the box

 Using a hammer and nail. punch two holes in the front of the sled. Then tie a piece of yarn to the sled

YOU'RE DONE!

33

//// With temperatures dropping and night approaching, building your own shelter is essential. But this isn't your normal ice igloo. Yours will be made from cardboard!

PROJECT #2

IGLOO

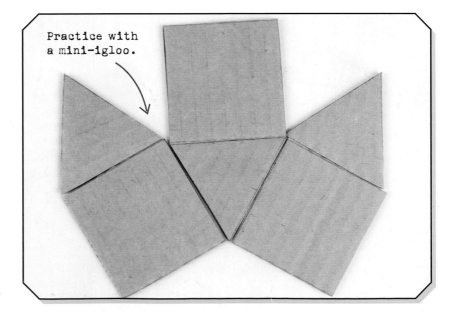

SUPPLIES

- large corrugated cardboard boxes
- scissors
- duct tape
- craft knife (or box cutter)
- cutting mat
- ruler
- tape measure
- paint and paintbrush

1. Cut out three equilateral triangles and three squares. An equilateral triangle's sides are all the same length.

Practice with a mini-igloo.

2 Trim duct tape to fit. Tape the pieces together in the arrangement shown below. (steps 2-4 are using a small-scale model)

 3 Attach the two side triangles to the square in between them. Your igloo should now be completely formed.

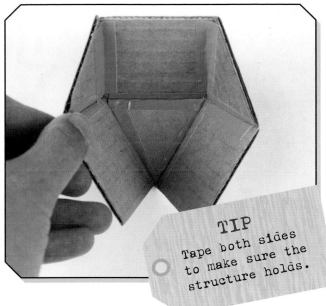

TIP
Tape both sides to make sure the structure holds.

 4 Decorate the igloo with more duct tape or paint.

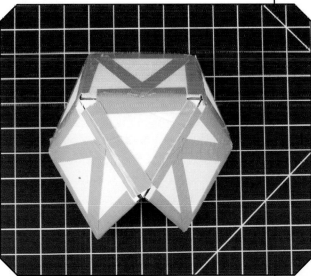

After you've finished using your cardboard igloo, fold it along the seams and pack it away!

HOW LONG SHOULD YOUR PIECES BE?

Well, that depends on your height! Sit down and have someone measure your height seated. You'll need to be able to sit inside your igloo. For an igloo to fit a person who is 26-32 inches (66–81 cm) tall, your pieces must have sides that are between 30-37 inches (76–94 cm) long. Try adding around 5 inches (13 cm) to your seated height, and that should do the trick!

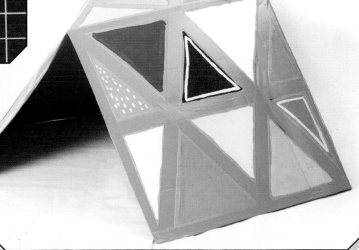

PROJECT #3

SNOWSHOES

Brr! How do arctic explorers travel over snow without sinking in? They wear snowshoes! Craft your very own pair of rad snow kicks from cardboard with this fun, wearable craft!

SUPPLIES

- paper for template
- corrugated cardboard

- shoe
- pencil
- scissors

- craft knife
- cutting mat
- tacky glue

- duct tape (orange, silver, yellow)
- clear tape

1 Trace around your shoe to make a template for your snowshoes. Cut out your template.

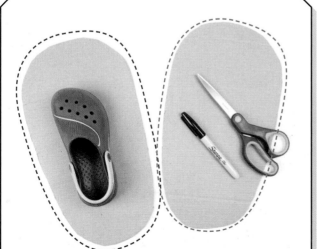

2 Use your template to make four same-sized shoe pieces from the corrugated cardboard. Each snowshoe will be made by stacking two of your shoe pieces on top of each other.

LEFT SHOE

Piece 1

Piece 2

RIGHT SHOE

Piece 3

Piece 4

TIP
You could make only one shoe piece per foot, but your shoes won't be as strong!

Use a craft knife and cutting mat to cut out a slit on each side of the cardboard around your shoe. Place that piece on top of another shoe shape and mark the slits. Now cut out those slits. Glue the two shoe shapes together.

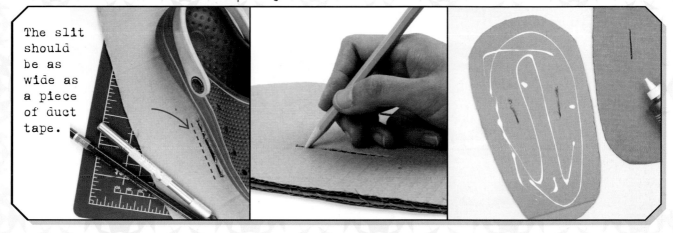

The slit should be as wide as a piece of duct tape.

 Cut out small pieces of duct tape and wrap them around both pieces. Cut out designs from duct tape and decorate the shoe base.

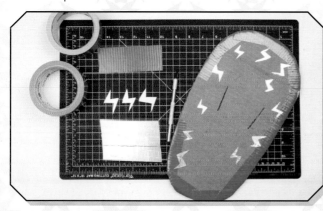

 (To make top strap)

Cut out two similar-sized duct tape pieces to span over your foot.

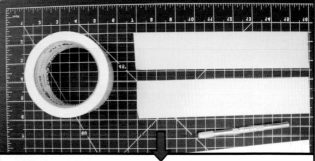

Flip one piece of clear tape so it's sticky-side up. Use a piece of tape to hold it down. Then place the other piece of tape on top.

Tape it to the bottom of your shoe.

 (To make back strap)

Cut out a piece of duct tape that will go around the back of your foot. Fold the duct tape in half to make a thin strap. Tape it to your top strap.

TRAVEL

Medieval
Defense

The Wild West

Ninja

THROUGH **TIME**

Prehistoric

DINOSAURS

What would it be like to live during the time of dinosaurs? Hop into your time machine and find out!

PREHISTORIC

- corrugated cardboard
- scissors
- drill
- paint and paintbrush
- permanent markers
- metal fasteners

Cut your dinosaur bodies, arms, and legs from cardboard.

Cut out slits in the legs and bodies to connect them later.

2 Drill a hole through each arm and dinosaur body to make arms that move.

TIP
Make sure your adult helper operates (or helps you operate) the drill!

3 Paint your dinosaurs. Use markers to add extra details that make your prehistoric beasts pop.

For a fun contrast, try painting one side like a skeleton and the other side normally.

4 Fasten the arms to the bodies. Slide the leg pieces in. You're all set!

PROJECT #2

PTERODACTYL COSTUME

How would you like to fly as high as a pterodactyl? Create your own prehistoric costume and soar as high as your imagination!

SUPPLIES

- cereal box
- scissors
- stapler
- pencil
- ruler
- cutting mat
- paint and paintbrush
- permanent markers
- duct tape
- corrugated cardboard
- drill (or hammer and nail)
- 2 pipe cleaners
- craft knife

STEPS FOR HEAD

 Cut out two strips from a cereal box.

 Staple one strip to go around your head and the other to go over your head.

3

Draw three similar-sized, connected triangles for the pterodactyl's face. Cut the triangles along the outline. Use your scissors to score the dotted connecting lines. Bend the cardboard along those lines.

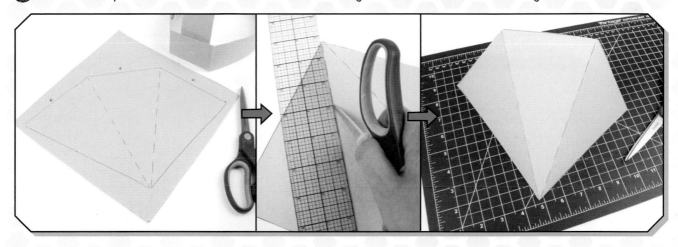

4 (To make and attach the back piece)

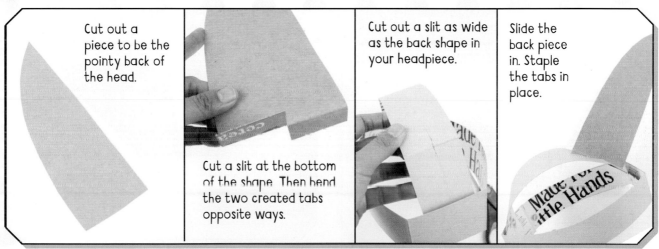

Cut out a piece to be the pointy back of the head.

Cut a slit at the bottom of the shape. Then bend the two created tabs opposite ways.

Cut out a slit as wide as the back shape in your headpiece.

Slide the back piece in. Staple the tabs in place.

5 Staple the face in front.

6 Paint your headpiece. Add details using permanent markers and duct tape.

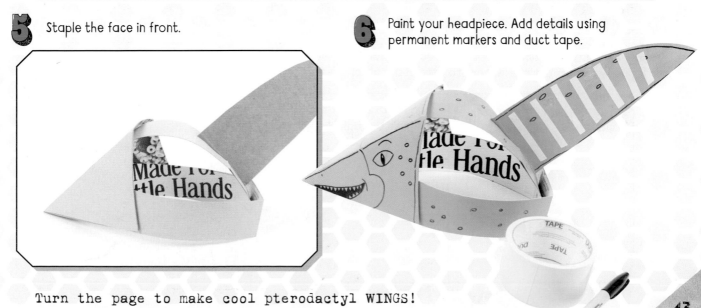

Turn the page to make cool pterodactyl WINGS!

Cut out a rectangle from corrugated cardboard that will fit on your back.

 Cut out this wing shape for both arms.

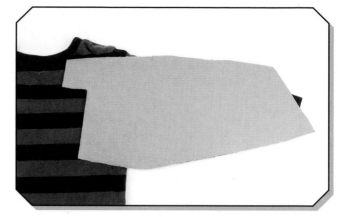

 Cut out four small rectangles to act as the fasteners. Now you should have two wing pieces, four small rectangles, and one back-sized rectangle.

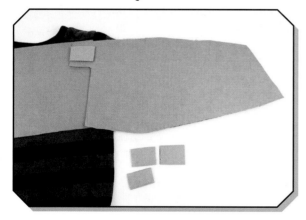

 Drill two holes in your back piece, one hole in each of your wings, and two holes in all four of your small rectangle fasteners.

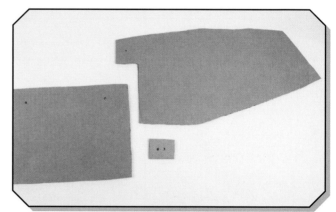

 Practice attaching your wings to make sure your cardboard fasteners work. Repeat these steps to attach the other wing.

Slide both ends of a pipe cleaner through the two holes of a small rectangle.

Slide both ends of the pipe cleaner through the wing and the back piece.

Slide the pipe cleaner ends through the two holes of another small rectangle. Twist them together.

6 Straighten the wings and use a line to mark the location of your shoulders.

 7 Cut along the line for both wings.

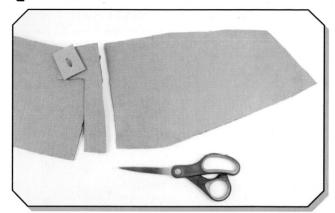

 8 Take everything apart and decorate your wings with paint, markers, and duct tape.

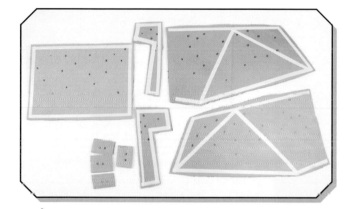

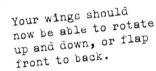 Your wings should now be able to rotate up and down, or flap front to back.

 9 Tape all wing pieces back together. Reattach the wings to the back piece using the fasteners (see step 11 for details.).

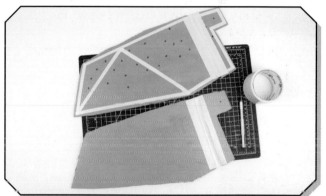

 10 To make your straps, cut out a long strip of duct tape. Turn it sticky-side up. Fold over one side so the strip is now half as thick. Make as many strips as you need. Use duct tape to attach two strips together to form four loops.

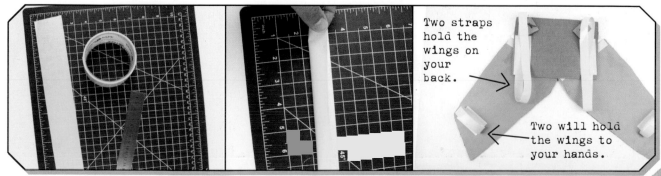

Two straps hold the wings on your back.

Two will hold the wings to your hands.

PROJECT #3

TIME MACHINE

They say time only moves forward. Well, it's time to break the rules! Travel back in time with your own time machine! Which time period will you visit?

SUPPLIES

- cardboard box
- paint and paintbrush
- duct tape
- scissors
- aluminum pie plate
- pencil
- corrugated cardboard
- construction paper

- glue (glue stick, hot glue, or tacky glue)
- permanent markers
- drill
- pipe cleaner
- additional items: colander, CD covers, stickers, clothespins, baking tray, magnetic numbers, egg beaters, pushpins, CDs, string of lights

1 Decorate your box with a coat of paint and strips of duct tape.

2 (To make the power meter)
Cut out a portion from your pie plate. Trace your pie plate onto a piece of corrugated cardboard. Add on a rectangle, and then cut it out. Now you have a lever! Glue construction paper over half of your lever.

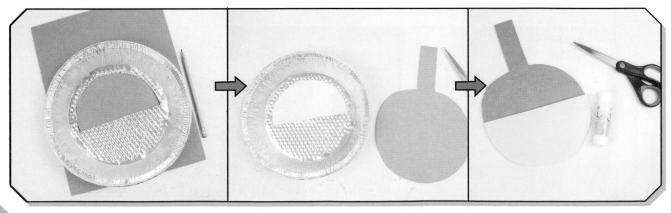

3 **(To attach the power meter)**
Drill two holes in the box where you want to place the power meter. Then drill two holes through the center of your pie pan and one hole through your lever. Wind the two ends of your pipe cleaner through the pie pan. Then twist the pipe cleaner. Slide the pipe cleaner through the lever. Then slide the ends through the two holes in the box. Twist the pipe cleaner ends together.

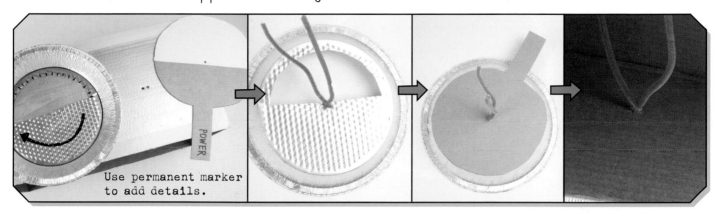

Use permanent marker
to add details.

POWER

4 **(To decorate your time machine)**

Use a colander to
hold wires.

Tape on
CD covers.

Tape on a baking
tray for a screen.

Add magnetic
numbers to set
the date.

Drill holes for items like egg
beaters to sit in place.

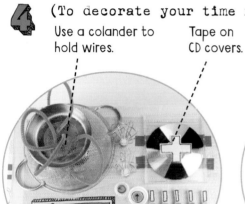

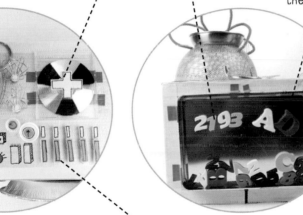

Use markers and stickers
to add on details.

Decorate clothespins
with duct tape.

Use pushpins to hang
CDs from the box.

 5 **(To add lights)**
Add lights by cutting out
holes in the box. Then
pull lights through and
turn them on!

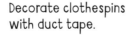

SWORD AND SHIELD

Hark all ye noble knights! Grab your swords and shields! It's time to rally behind your king and queen to protect your land and people. Let's put your cardboard crafting skills to work and create this sword and shield pair.

SUPPLIES

- paper
- pencil
- scissors
- corrugated cardboard

- duct tape (silver, gold, bronze, black)
- craft knife
- cutting mat
- tacky glue

- paint (black, red, white) and paintbrush
- permanent marker

STEPS FOR SWORD

Create a template for your sword and handle. Use it to trace and cut out three swords from cardboard.

2 Tape your swords together. Cut out strips of duct tape and wrap the sword's blade.

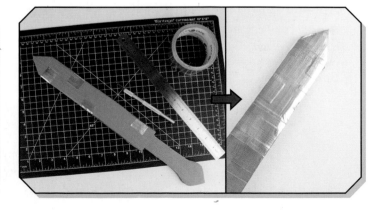

3 Now let's make the sword's guard. Cut out a rectangle with a hole in it. The hole should be large enough to fit the sword handle through. Cover it with duct tape and slide it on over your sword.

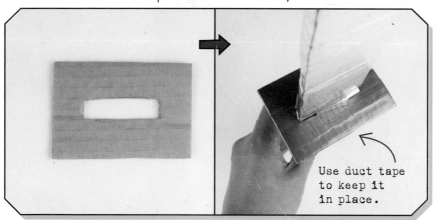

Use duct tape to keep it in place.

 4 Now wrap the bottom of the handle with duct tape.

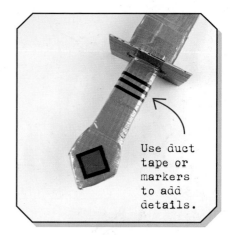

Use duct tape or markers to add details.

STEPS FOR SHIELD

 1 Create a template for a shield. Then trace and cut out two shields from cardboard.

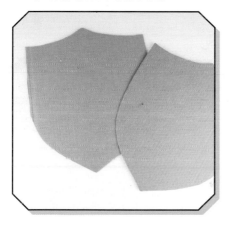

 2 Use tacky glue to stick them both together.

TIP
Put the shields under a heavy book to help them glue together tightly.

 3 Once your glue dries, paint the shield. Then use permanent markers to add detail.

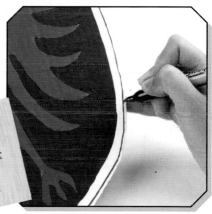

 4 Cut out two thin strips from corrugated cardboard.

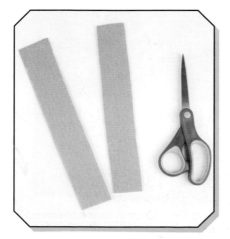

 5 Bend the strips to create handles.

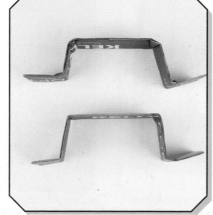

6 Use tape to attach the handles to the back of the shield.

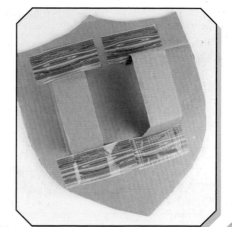

PROJECT #2
ROYAL CROWN

It's time to tap into your royal side. Call forth your inner monarch with an awesome duct tape crown!

SUPPLIES

- gold duct tape
- craft knife
- cutting mat
- clear tape
- ruler
- pencil
- cereal box
- scissors
- permanent markers
- stapler

1 Cut strips of duct tape and overlap them on top of each other until you have a crown height that you like.

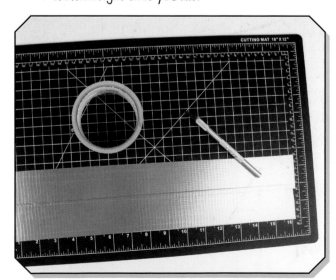

2 Lift up your strips of duct tape. Turn them sticky-side up. Tape them down with clear tape to hold them in place.

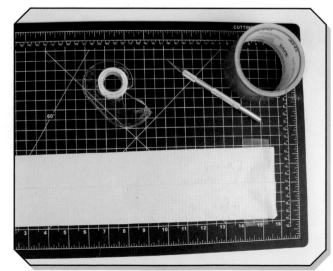

Cover the sticky duct tape with other
duct tape strips.

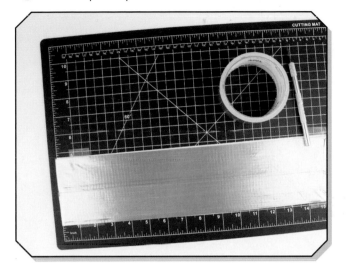

 Use a ruler and pencil to sketch a crown shape
onto a cereal box. This can be used as a template.

 Repeat steps 1–3 to make more of these crown
strips. Then use duct tape to tape them together.

 Add extra details with permanent markers
and duct tape.

 Staple the crown together and then
trim off any excess duct tape.

PROJECT #3

KNIGHT'S HELMET

All great knights need a strong helmet to protect them in battle. Craft your own from duct tape and cardboard in no time!

SUPPLIES

- scissors
- several pieces of cereal box cardboard
- yarn
- ruler
- duct tape
- craft knife
- cutting mat
- stapler
- pencil
- paper (for template)

Cut open your cereal box. Cut out a cardboard rectangle that is big enough to wrap around your head.

TIP
Unsure of your size? Wrap a piece of yarn around your head. Add 2 inches (5 cm) to that length. That will be the length of your cardboard piece.

2 Once you are sure of the fit, cover one side with duct tape.

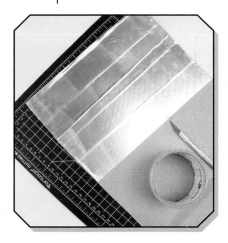

 3 Curl your cardboard into a tube. Staple it together.

Cover the staples with small pieces of duct tape.

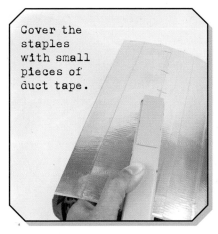

 4 Trace around your cylinder on a piece of cereal box.

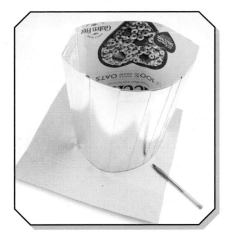

 5 Cut out the traced shape.

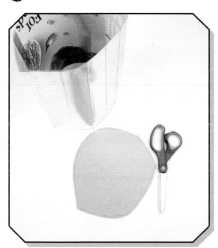

 6 Cover the shape with duct tape.

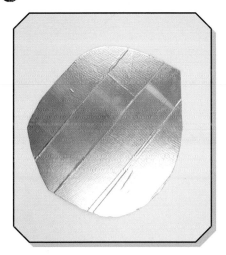

 7 Attach the shape to the top of your helmet.

Use small pieces of duct tape to do this.

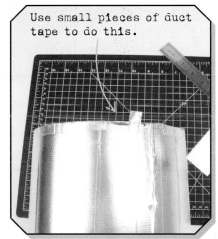

 8 Cut out openings for your eyes and nose.

You can free hand this, or create your own template.

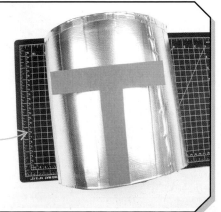

 9 Add extra details with duct tape.

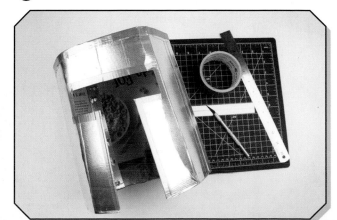

PROJECT #1

PIRATE HAT

Arrr, matey! What does every pirate need? A sturdy hat, of course! Grab some cardboard and make your own faster than you can say, "walk the plank!"

ARRR!

- tape measure
- paper
- cereal box
- permanent marker
- scissors
- paint and paintbrush
- stapler

Measure the circumference of your head. Draw a line of the same length on paper. Then create a template for your hat with that line as the bottom.

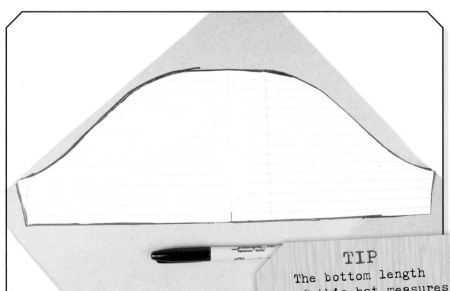

TIP
The bottom length of this hat measures 14½ inches (37 cm) and would fit a 6-year-old child.

Trace your template onto a piece of cereal box cardboard two times. Cut out both pieces.

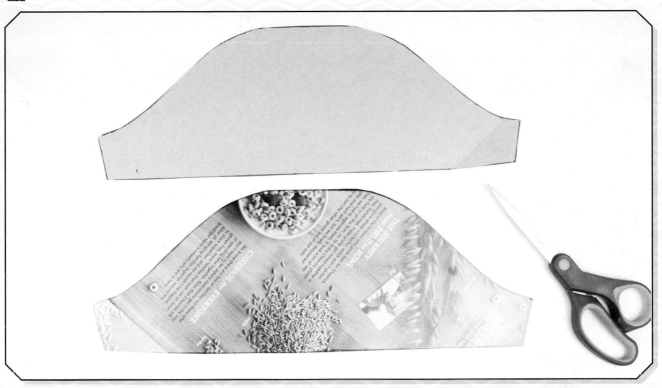

 Paint the pieces and let them dry.

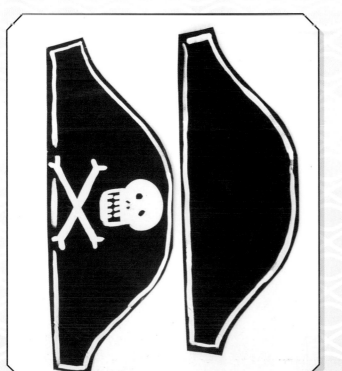

4 Staple the pieces together so they fit your head. You're all done, Captain!

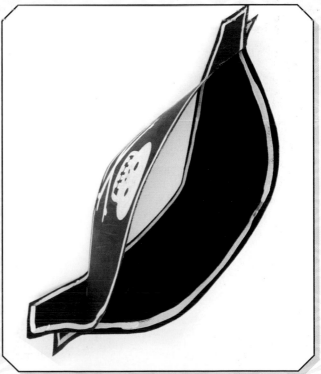

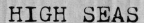

PROJECT #2

AIR CANNONS

Look out there in the distance. A warring enemy ship is coming your way! It's time to ready the cannons and fight. Grab your cardboard and make your own air cannon!

SUPPLIES

- cutting mat
- scissors or craft knife
- oatmeal container

- duct tape
- permanent markers
- toilet paper rolls

- cardboard box

STEPS FOR OATMEAL AIR CANNON

1. Cut a hole in the bottom of your oatmeal container.

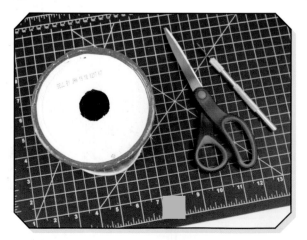

2. Duct tape the lid onto your container. Make sure there are no holes.

3 Use permanent markers and duct tape to add details. Decorate toilet paper rolls as targets.

Aim at your targets and give the container a firm squeeze. Watch the air knock them down!

STEPS FOR BOX AIR CANNON

 1 Cut a hole in the front of your box. Tape the box closed.

 2 Make sure to seal up all corners and holes with duct tape so air can only escape through the hole.

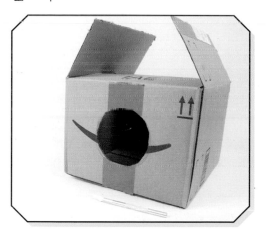

Hold the box between your hands and firmly push inward to knock your targets down with a strong gust of air!

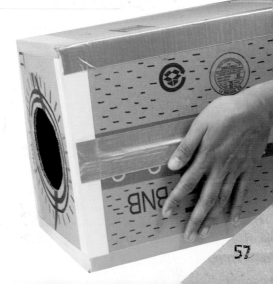

57

PROJECT #3

TREASURE CHEST

Looking for a place to stash yer treasure? Grab a shoe box and some duct tape and make yourself a treasure chest fit to hold all yer loot!

 (To make the treasure chest lid) Cut off one of the long back panels from a shoe box lid.

 Cut out two identical trapezoids from cereal box cardboard.

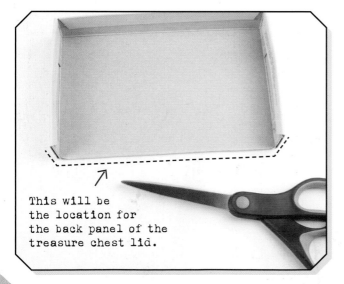

This will be the location for the back panel of the treasure chest lid.

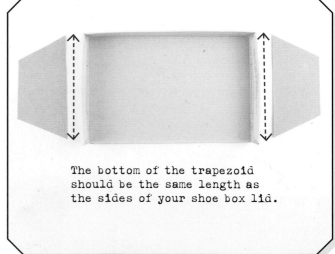

The bottom of the trapezoid should be the same length as the sides of your shoe box lid.

Cut out three rectangular pieces to be the top of the treasure chest. They should all be the same length as the shoe box lid.

 Use duct tape to assemble the top of the treasure chest. The three rectangular pieces should be sandwiched between the trapezoid pieces. The top should now sit neatly on top of the shoe box lid.

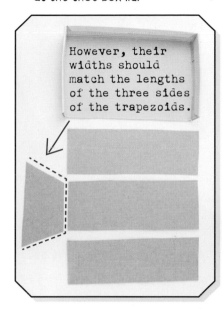

However, their widths should match the lengths of the three sides of the trapezoids.

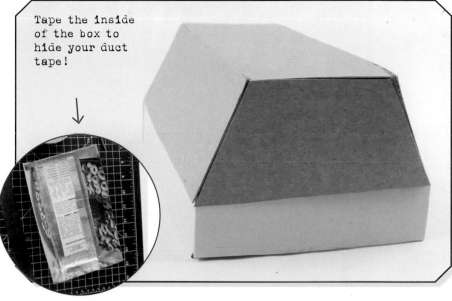

Tape the inside of the box to hide your duct tape!

 Paint the bottom sides of the shoe box. Then paint the sides and top of the lid.

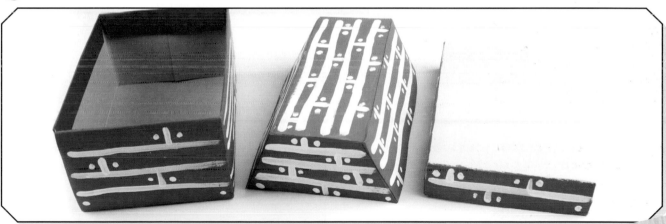

 Use duct tape to attach the treasure chest top to the shoe box lid. Then use duct tape to attach the back of the shoe box lid to the chest to create a "hinge." Now you have a treasure chest!

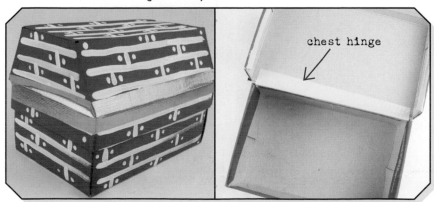

chest hinge

TIP

Short on time? You can quickly create a container to store your treasures! Simply paint an egg carton and add some gold duct tape.

PROJECT #1
NUNCHUCKS

To become a ninja, you have to have awesome combat skills. How about learning with some sweet new nunchucks? Grab your cardboard and duct tape, and start your training now!

Hiyya!

SUPPLIES

- black and silver duct tape
- 4 toilet paper rolls
- cutting mat
- craft knife (to trim duct tape)
- hole punch
- yarn

1 Tape two toilet paper rolls to each other.

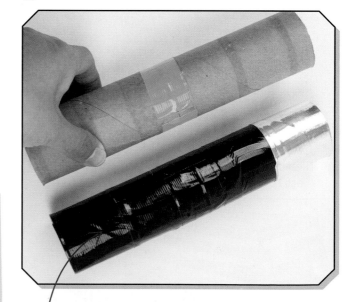

2 Cut out 6½-inch (17-cm) strips of black and silver duct tape. Use them to cover the toilet paper rolls.

TIP

Apply the black tape first. Cover the entire toilet paper roll by slightly overlapping each piece of tape.

Once both nunchucks are covered with duct tape, punch a hole into the top of each nunchuck. Use a piece of yarn to tie both nunchucks together.

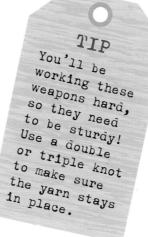

TIP

You'll be working these weapons hard, so they need to be sturdy! Use a double or triple knot to make sure the yarn stays in place.

 To give the yarn a metallic look, cut out thin strips of silver duct tape. Roll the strips onto different sections of the yarn.

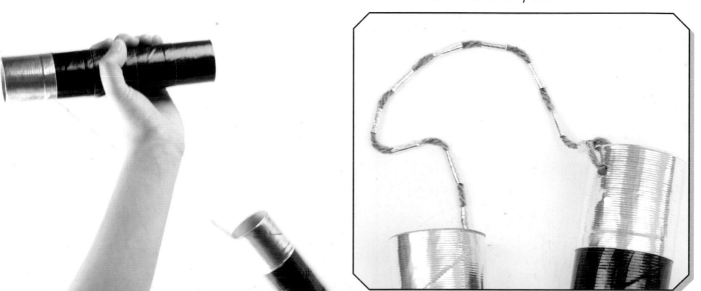

PROJECT #2
NINJA SWORD

As a ninja, your sword can serve as your best friend. With one swift movement, the innocent are protected and foes are conquered. Craft your very own sword from cardboard!

SUPPLIES

- black, gold, and silver duct tape
- toilet paper roll
- paper towel roll
- pencil and paper
- corrugated cardboard
- pencil
- scissors
- cutting mat
- craft knife

1 (To make the sword's sheath) Tape a toilet paper roll to a paper towel roll.

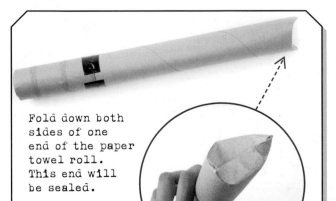

Fold down both sides of one end of the paper towel roll. This end will be sealed.

2 Carefully wrap strips of black duct tape around the long tube. When everything is covered, add details with gold duct tape.

(To make the sword)
Draw a sword template on paper. Use it as a template to cut out three to four identical swords from cardboard.

Make sure the swords fit into the sheath.

4 To make a thicker sword, tape two sword pieces together. Cover the new sword with strips of duct tape.

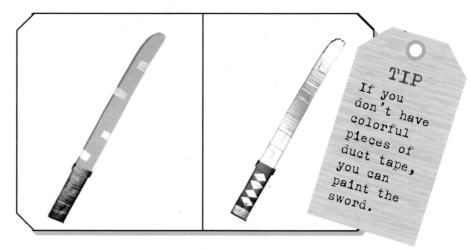

TIP
If you don't have colorful pieces of duct tape, you can paint the sword.

 (To make the sword's collar)
Cut out two identical pieces of cardboard. Make a rectangular cutout in the middle.

This cutout should be just big enough for the sword to slide through.

 Tape both pieces of cardboard together. Then cover with duct tape. Trim the tape with a craft knife. Attach the collar to the sword by sliding it over the blade. Secure it to the sword with more tape.

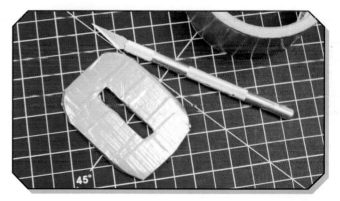

 (To make the shoulder strap)
Cut out a 16-inch (41-cm) strip of duct tape. Lay it on a cutting board sticky-side up. Fold over one-third of the strip. Then fold over another third. Make another one, and tape the two together to make a long strap. Tape both ends onto the sheath.

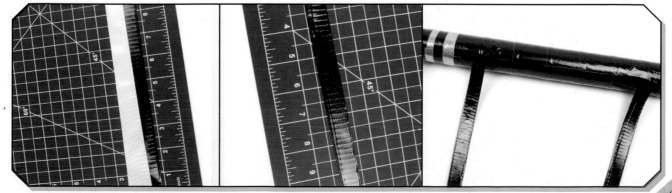

PROJECT #3
DAGGERS

With enemies all around, how would you defend yourself in ancient Japan? These cardboard daggers should do the trick. Small and sleek, these weapons are perfect for whipping out and surprising opponents.

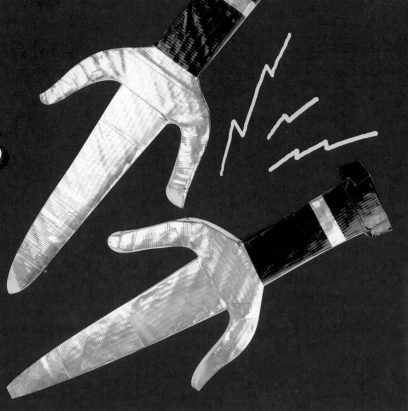

- permanent marker and paper
- scissors
- corrugated cardboard
- pencil
- duct tape
- craft knife
- cutting mat

 Draw and cut out a template for a dagger.

2 Trace it onto a piece of cardboard. Cut out.

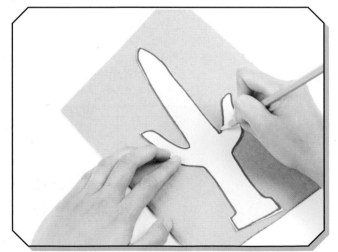

3 Do this three more times to make four identical daggers.

TIP

Each dagger is made using two cardboard daggers. Doubling the cardboard makes the daggers sturdier.

 4 To make each dagger, tape two cardboard blades together.

 5 Wrap the daggers with strips of duct tape.

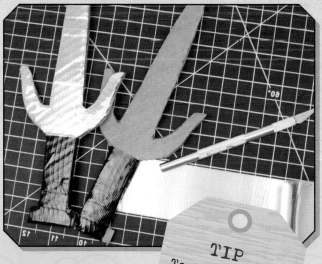

TIP

To make sure the cardboard will be completely covered, overlap the tape as you wrap the dagger.

RUBBER BAND GUN

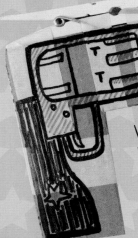

Whizz! Did you see that rubber band just fly by? You can use this craft to protect yourself and the innocent as you explore the wild west!

SUPPLIES

- corrugated cardboard
- scissors
- craft stick
- masking tape
- clothespin
- rubber bands
- permanent markers

TIP
The length of your gun should be about as long as the length of a stretched rubber band plus the length of a clothespin.

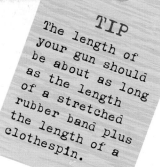

1 Cut out two identical gun shapes. Both should have tiny slits in identical locations. The slits will be spots for the rubber bands to slide into.

slits

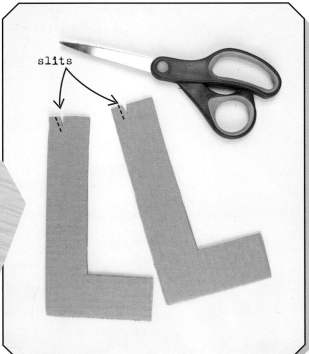

2 Tape a craft stick to one gun cutout. This will ensure that your gun does not bend.

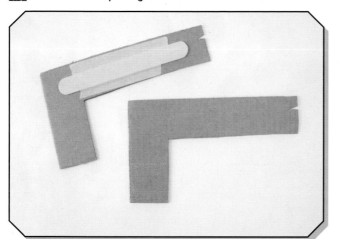

 3 Tape both cardboard shapes together, sandwiching the craft stick in between.

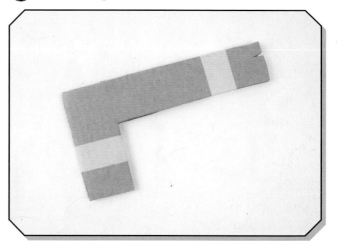

 4 Tape the clothespin to the top of the gun. The rubber band should be taut when stretched and held by the clothespin. When released, it should fly across the room. If it doesn't work, adjust your design accordingly.

TIP
Use a stretched rubber band to test out where you should tape the clothespin.

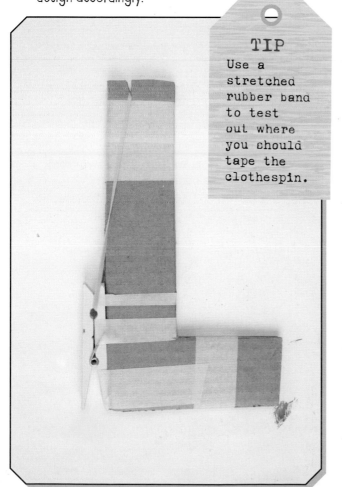

 5 Once you have a working rubber band gun, add details with permanent markers!

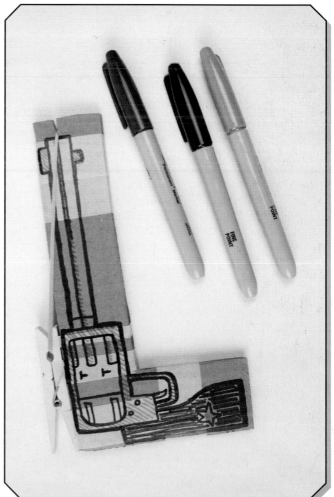

PROJECT #2

SHERIFF'S VEST

Are you ready to protect and serve? With this sheriff's vest, you'll strike fear in the hearts of thieves and bandits roaming the Wild West. You'll restore the land to order!

SUPPLIES

- T-shirt
- permanent markers
- ruler
- fabric scissors
- cutting mat
- duct tape
- craft knife

1 On your shirt, sketch out where you're going to cut. You'll need two front panels and one back panel.

2 Use fabric scissors to cut out the two front panels and back panel of your vest.

two front panels

one back panel

Don't forget to cut out and discard the sleeves.

TIP Fabric scissors are made for cutting fabric. If you don't own a pair, regular scissors will work fine!

3 Cover your fabric panels with strips of duct tape.

4 Lift the covered fabric off the mat and flip over.

5 Trim off the excess duct tape.

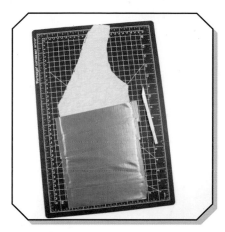

6 To decorate the vest, use a craft knife to cut out different shapes and strips of duct tape. Attach them to the vest.

7 To create fringe, cut out a strip of duct tape. Place it sticky-side up. Then fold up a portion of the duct tape. Leave a little bit of the sticky side revealed. Then use scissors to cut out fringe and attach it to the vest.

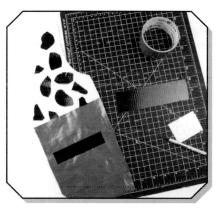

8 Use pieces of duct tape to attach the front two panels to the back panel. Now you can wear your sheriff's vest!

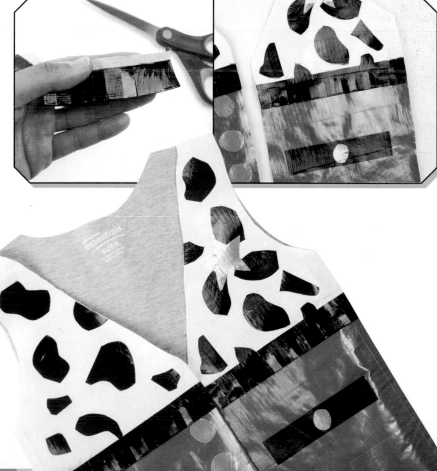

PROJECT #3

COWBOY SPURS

Cowboys share a special relationship with their horses. To get the horses going, they often use spurs. Metal spurs are worn over boots. Make your own spurs from duct tape and cardboard!

SUPPLIES

- corrugated cardboard
- scissors
- drill (or hammer and nail)
- pair of boots
- stapler
- duct tape
- craft knife
- cutting mat
- yarn

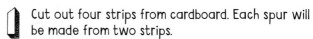

Cut out four strips from cardboard. Each spur will be made from two strips.

Make sure the strips extend from the front of your foot to beyond your ankle.

2 Ask an adult to drill a hole through one side of each strip.

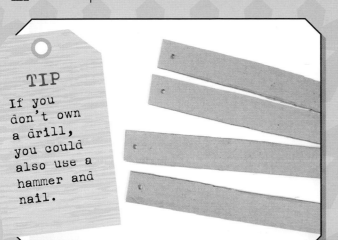

TIP
If you don't own a drill, you could also use a hammer and nail.

3 Take two strips and staple them together so they fit loosely around the ankle of your boot.

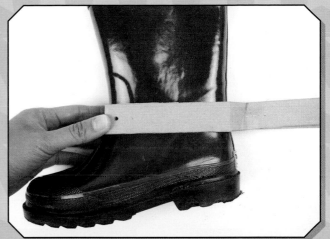

4 Add "metallic" detail with duct tape.

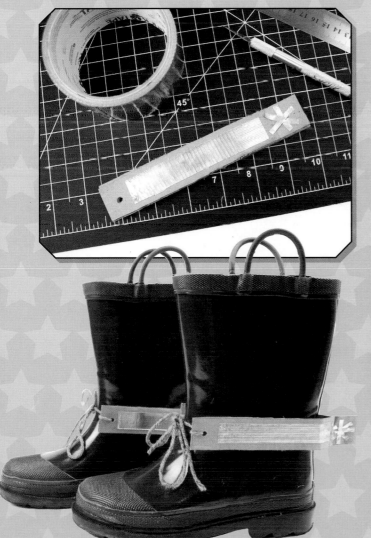

5 Cut two pieces of yarn, and use them to tie both sides of your spurs together. Do this for both spurs.

PUT ON

Lights, Camera, Action!

Magician

Carnival Fun

A SHOW

Rock Concert

PROJECT #1

TAMBOURINE

Nothings keeps the beat like the happy jingle of a tambourine. Start your very own band with this cardboard instrument keeping time!

- craft knife
- oatmeal container
- cutting mat
- lined paper
- hole punch
- duct tape
- permanent markers
- paint and paintbrush
- pipe cleaners
- bells

Using a craft knife, cut out a ring of cardboard around the lid of an oatmeal container. Save the rest of the container for the crafts on pages 78-79!)

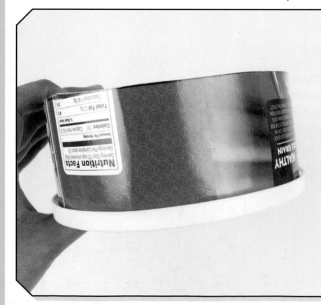

An easy way to make sure your ring is even is to cut out a rectangle from lined paper. Line it up against the edge of your container and trace around the paper for a line to follow while cutting.

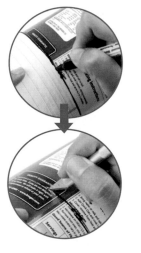

Use a hole punch to punch pairs of holes around the cardboard cylinder.

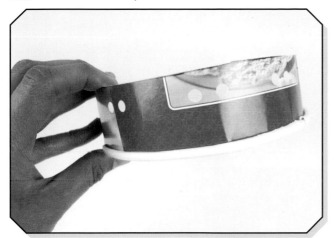

 Use duct tape and permanent markers to decorate the lid (face) of the tambourine.

 Paint the cardboard cylinder. Once the paint dries, attach the lid.

 Use pipe cleaners to attach bells to the outside of the tambourine.

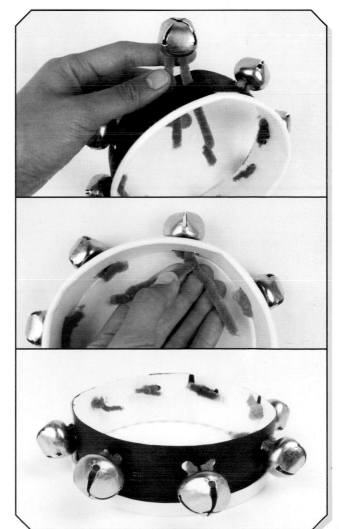

PROJECT #2
DRUM SET

Every good band needs a drummer. Without one, who would keep the beat? Create your own drum set with tin cans and boxes, and pound your way to an awesome rock concert!

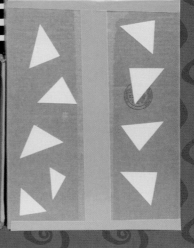

SUPPLIES

- cardboard boxes in various sizes
- duct tape
- scissors

- used tin cans in various sizes
- cork from a bottle

- disposable aluminum pie plates
- pushpins

- drill (or hammer and nail)
- yarn
- chopsticks

---

1 Tape a cardboard box shut. Decorate it with shapes cut from the different-sized boxes.

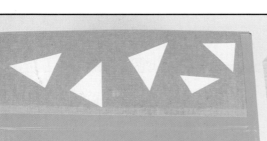

TIP
You can also use stickers, crayons, or markers to decorate your boxes.

2 To make a tin can "cowbell," wash and dry the can. Decorate it with duct tape.

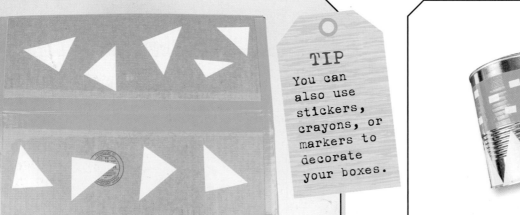

3 (To make a cymbal and stand)

Attach a cork to the top of a cardboard box. Attach a pie plate to the top with a pushpin. Use duct tape to tape the box shut. Then decorate it.

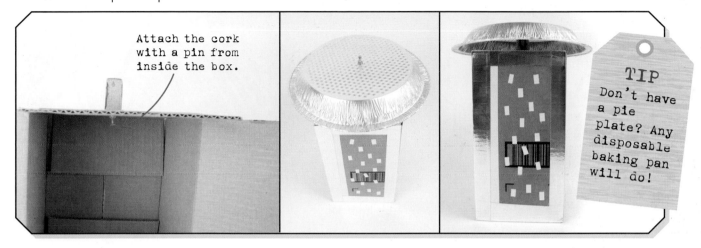

Attach the cork with a pin from inside the box.

TIP
Don't have a pie plate? Any disposable baking pan will do!

4 (To make tin can "bells")

Wash your tin cans well. Drill two holes in the bottom of each can. For each can you plan on using, drill two corresponding holes in your cardboard box. Use pieces of yarn to tie the cans to the inside of your box. Decorate your box and cans with duct tape.

5 Arrange your various instruments, and play them with chopsticks!

TIP
Don't own chopsticks? Use pencils, markers, or any long sturdy sticks instead!

Don't forget to decorate and seal other boxes to join your set!

PROJECT #3
BANJO AND UKULELE

Ready to transform the leftover oatmeal container into not just one, but two stringed instruments? Time to make a banjo and ukulele and get your band playing!

SUPPLIES

- scissors
- leftover oatmeal container (from pages 74–75)
- pencil
- 2 cereal boxes
- corrugated cardboard
- tacky glue

- craft knife
- cutting mat
- paint and paintbrush
- permanent marker
- drill (or hammer and nail)
- 8 rubber bands
- duct tape

STEPS FOR UKULELE

1 (To make the body) Cut out two cardboard rings of similar width from the oatmeal container.

TIP
Save the bottom of the oatmeal container to make the banjo!

To make a ring that is uniformly wide, refer to step 1 on page 74.

2 Place one ring on top of the other so they overlap a little bit. Mark the two places where the rings overlap. Cut two slits where you marked the cardboard. Slide the two rings together to create a ukulele frame.

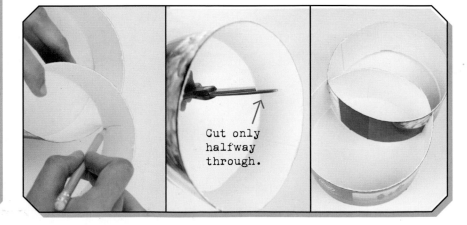

Cut only halfway through.

3 Trace your frame onto a piece of cereal box cardboard two times. Cut out. One piece will be the back of your instrument. One will be the front. Cut out a small hole from the front of your ukulele.

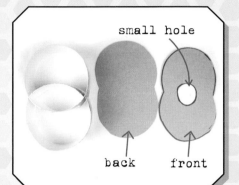

small hole

back   front

 4 Cut out two small rectangles from cardboard. They should be about 2 inches (5 cm) long.

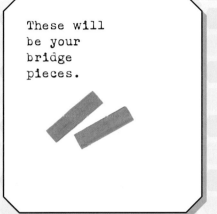

These will be your bridge pieces.

 5 Cut out two long rectangles from cardboard. They should be about 9 inches (23 cm) long. Glue the two pieces together.

This is the fingerboard.

 6 Use a craft knife to cut a hole in the top of the frame.

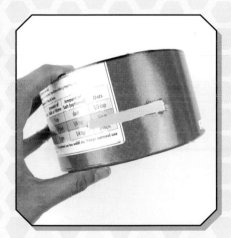

 7 Glue the back of the ukulele to the frame.

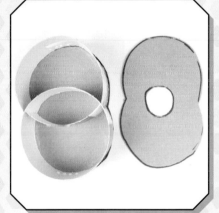

 8 Now you can decorate your ukulele parts with paint and marker.

 9 Glue on the two bridge pieces.

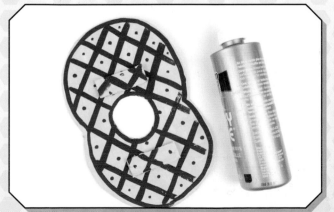

 10 Ask an adult to drill four holes on top and below the bridge pieces.

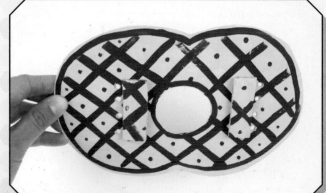

ROCK CONCERT

11 Cut four rubber bands in half. Tie them together and push the other ends through two top holes. Then stretch the bands over the sound hole and push them through the two bottom corresponding holes. Tie the rubber bands together to hold them in place. Do the same process for the remaining pairs of holes.

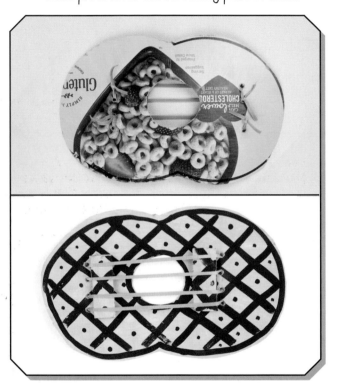

12 Push the cardboard rectangle through the hole. Carefully tear apart the two pieces of cardboard for about ½ inch (1.3 cm). Tape it to the inside of the instrument.

Don't forget to attach the front of the ukulele with tacky glue. Now you're ready to play!

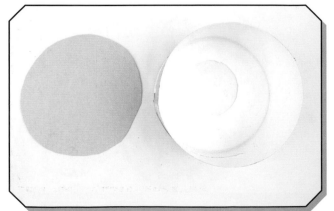

STEPS FOR BANJO

1 Cut out a circle in the oatmeal container's bottom piece. This will be the opening in the banjo.

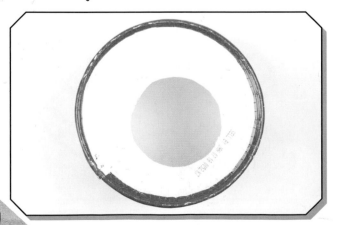

2 Trace the banjo body onto a piece of cereal box. Cut out the resulting circle. This will be the back of your banjo.

(Make the bridge and fingerboard pieces)

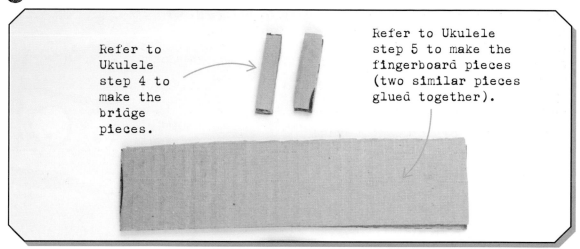

Refer to Ukulele step 4 to make the bridge pieces.

Refer to Ukulele step 5 to make the fingerboard pieces (two similar pieces glued together).

4 Use a marker or paint to decorate all of the banjo parts.

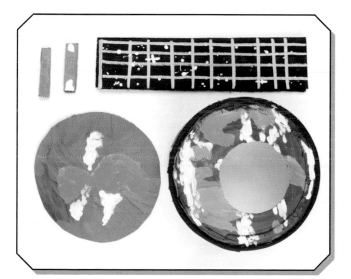

5 Glue one bridge piece on top of the cutout circle. Glue the other bridge piece just below the cutout circle. Ask an adult to drill four holes on top and four holes on the bottom of the banjo head.

6 String your banjo as shown in Ukulele step 11.

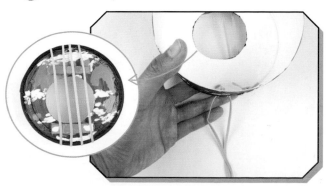

7 Attach the fingerboard as shown in Ukulele step 12. Now get playing!

PROJECT #1

BOX PUPPETS

Have some small boxes you don't know what to do with? Turn them into talking hand puppets with big personalities and big mouths!

- pencil
- ruler
- small corrugated boxes
- craft knife
- cutting mat
- paint and paintbrush
- permanent markers
- hot glue (or tacky glue)
- additional decorative items (construction paper, pom-poms, yarn, sequins, etc.)

1 Mark a line through the middle of the box.

2 Use a craft knife to cut along this line. Continue following the line and cut two more sides. One side of your box should remain intact — this allows the box to open on a hinge.

3 Stand your box up. The open side is where you'll use your fingers to operate the puppets. The other side will be the puppets' faces.

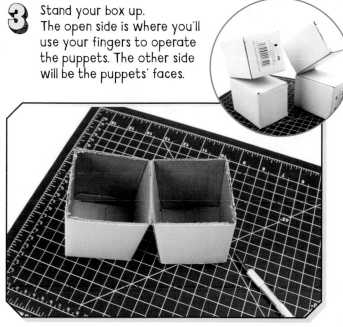

4 Decorate the puppets. Paint their faces and the insides of their mouths different colors.

Use permanent markers to add details.

5 Use pom-poms, construction paper, or other materials to add extra flair.

What? Speak up!

LA, LA, LA, LA, LA!

PROJECT #2

TUBE PUPPETS

Psst! Want to know the easiest way to make puppets? Use toilet paper rolls. These tubes are free and always lying around. Just grab a couple and you've got all the materials needed to make a fun cast of characters!

SUPPLIES

- toilet roll tubes
- paint and paintbrushes
- permanent markers
- craft knife
- cutting mat
- duct tape
- corrugated cardboard
- decorative papers
- glue stick

DECORATE TOILET PAPER TUBES IN THREE EASY WAYS:

FOLD DOWN TOPS

1

Fold down one edge of the tube.

2

Create "ears" by folding down the opposite edge over the first edge.

3
Add personalities by decorating with paint and permanent markers.

ADD PAPER OR DUCT TAPE STRIPS

1 Cut out strips of paper or duct tape.

2 Stick the strips to the tubes.

3 Use permanent markers to add details.

TIP
Want more ideas? Try transforming these tubes into owls, cats, dogs, bats, or even superheroes!

ADD MORE PIECES WITH SLOTS

1 Cut out slots in the cardboard tubes and other pieces of cardboard. Add details with paint, strips of paper, or duct tape.

2 Then simply slide pieces together to completely change the shape of your tubes.

PROJECT #3

SHADOW THEATER

Ever made shadow puppets with your hands? Well, with this fun craft, you'll tell shadow stories using cardboard, paper, and light!

SUPPLIES

- cardboard box
- ruler
- pencil
- craft knife
- cutting mat
- scissors
- paint and paintbrush
- parchment paper
- masking tape
- black construction paper
- white pencil
- skewers
- clear tape
- play dough
- strong flashlight or lamp
- optional: hole punch, markers, crayons, stickers

1 Draw a rectangle on the box. Try to keep a 1- to 2-inch (1.3- to 2.5-cm) border around the rectangle to ensure the box keeps its shape.

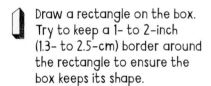

2 Cut out the rectangle.

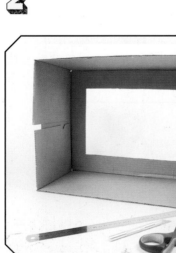

3 Decorate the outside of the box with paint (or whatever you'd like).

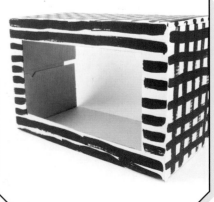

4 Cut out a piece of parchment paper to cover the box opening. Tape it in place.

TIP 1

Don't own parchment paper? Any thin, white paper will do.

5 Now let's make the puppets and backgrounds! Using a white pencil, draw your ideas on black construction paper.

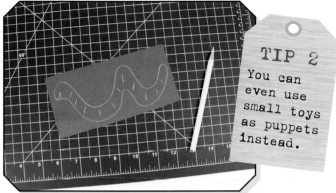

TIP 2

You can even use small toys as puppets instead.

6 Cut out the designs using scissors.

Create cutouts inside the designs using craft knives or a hole punch!

7 Tape puppets and backgrounds to skewers.

TIP 3

Try to tape your skewer so that it's hidden behind paper.

8 Let's set up our theater! Create little play dough "feet" for your background skewers. Then stand them up against the screen. Grab a flashlight or lamp and place it behind your theater. You'll then position your puppets between the theater and the light source. Now you're all set to put on a show!

Notice how the shadows change size and sharpness as you move your puppets nearer and farther from the light source.

TIP 4

If you don't plan to change backgrounds during your skit, simply tape your background to your screen instead of using skewers.

PROJECT #1

RING / CAP TOSS GAME

Step right up, it's time to play some games! Now you can make your own version of a ring toss or cap game with an egg carton and some duct tape. Who knew fun would be so easy?

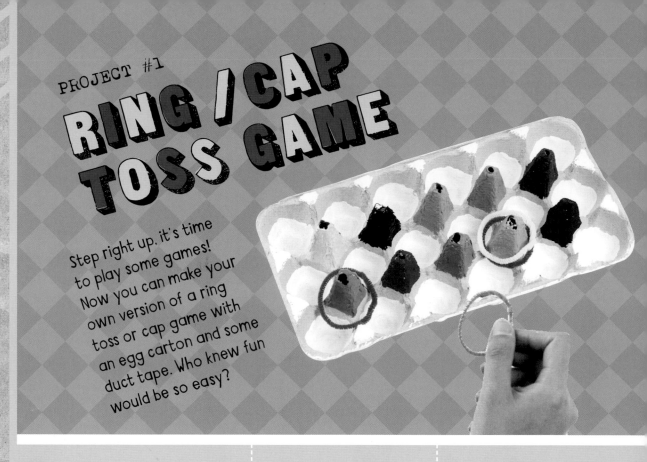

SUPPLIES

- 2 cardboard egg cartons
- paint and paintbrush
- scissors

- duct tape (or packing tape)
- hot glue (optional)
- pipe cleaners

- caps from squeeze pouches or milk jugs (or ping-pong balls)

1 Cut the lids off your egg cartons.

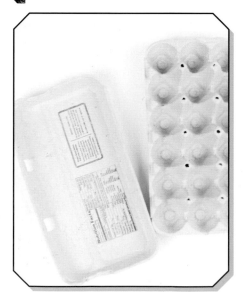

2 Paint your egg cartons.

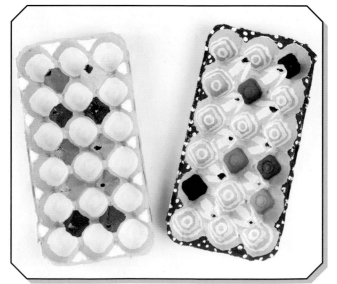

To make the Cap Toss game stand up, cut out three rectangular pieces from the egg carton lid. Tape them together to form a triangle.

 Hot glue your triangle to the back of your painted egg carton.

 To make the rings for the ring toss game, twist the two ends of the pipe cleaner together to form circles.

Try to get the cap in the colored portions of the egg carton! Toss the rings around the parts that stick up.

NOW START TOSSING!

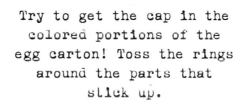

89

PROJECT #2

SHOOTING ARROWS

Not tired of games yet, are you? Because with this craft, you get to sling some arrows! No bows needed for this easy-to-make cardboard carnival game!

- scissors
- corrugated cardboard
- scissors
- permanent markers
- rubber band
- cereal box
- stapler

Cut out arrows from your corrugated cardboard and decorate them with markers.

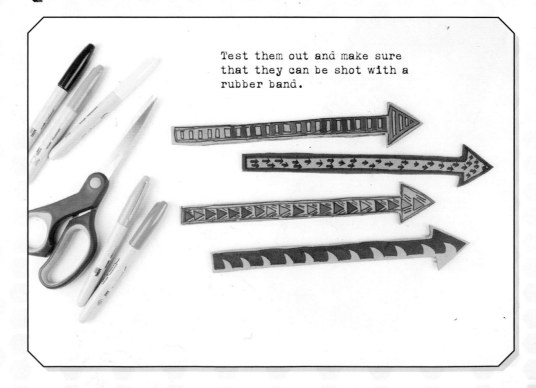

Test them out and make sure that they can be shot with a rubber band.

2 Let's create your bull's-eyes. Cut out rectangles from your cereal box. Fold them in half.

 3 Fold them in half again.

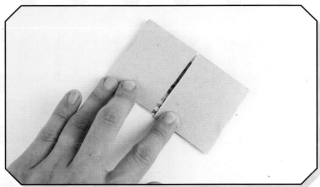

 4 Open up your folds and draw on a bull's-eye.

 5 Staple the bull's-eyes so they stand up.

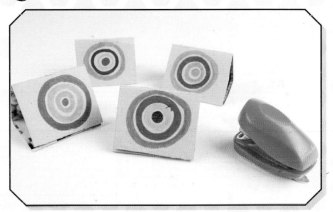

Stretch a rubber band between your thumb and pointer finger like a slingshot. Pull the arrow back and then let go! Did you hit your target?

PROJECT #3

SHOOTING DISK GAME

How good are you at shooting milk jug caps? This fun carnival game pits you against a partner. See how many caps you can shoot into this funny man's belly while an animated mustache blocks your moves!

SUPPLIES

- scissors
- craft knife
- cutting mat
- corrugated cardboard box
- corrugated cardboard
- ruler
- milk caps
- pencil
- drill (or hammer and nail)
- metal fastener
- paint and paintbrush
- permanent markers

Cut out a slot in both the front and back of your box. The slot should be big enough for a milk cap disk to easily slide through.

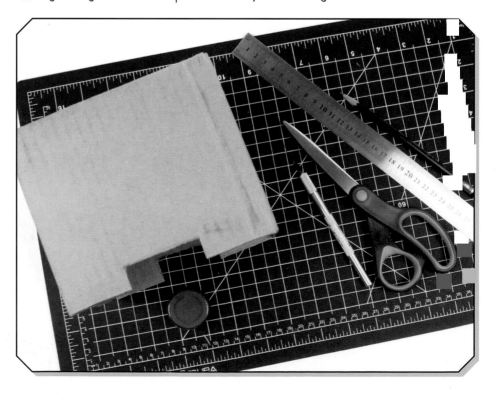

2 Cut out a mustache from corrugated cardboard.

3 Drill a hole in your box and mustache. The hole should be big enough to hold a fastener.

It should also be placed so that the mustache will effectively block caps.

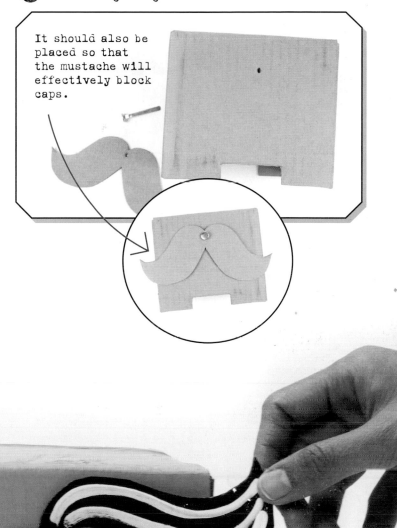

4 Use markers and paint to decorate your man.

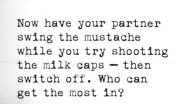

Now have your partner swing the mustache while you try shooting the milk caps — then switch off. Who can get the most in?

PROJECT #1

ACADEMY AWARDS

Did you write, act, or shoot a blockbuster movie? That's great! Let's celebrate your hard work and creativity with your very own award made of cardboard and duct tape!

- pencil and paper
- corrugated cardboard
- scissors
- tacky glue
- craft knife
- cutting mat
- small corrugated cardboard box
- black duct tape
- gold paint
- paintbrush
- permanent marker

1 Draw a template for your award. It should include a statue on top and a tab on the bottom. This will ensure that your statue slides into the award's base. Use your template to cut out three identical statues.

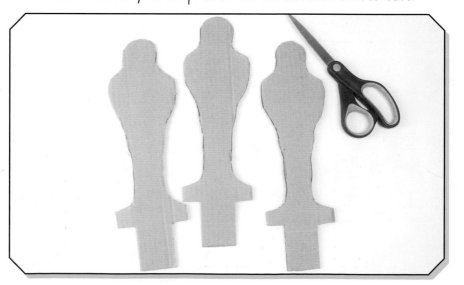

2 Use tacky glue to glue your cardboard pieces on top of each other.

3 Now we're going to make the base. Cut the bottom off a small box. Then cut out a slit in the middle of your box's top. Also cut out a piece of cardboard that is slightly larger than your base.

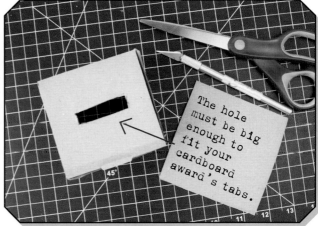

The hole must be big enough to fit your cardboard award's tabs.

4 Cover the two base pieces with black duct tape. You can also paint the base black.

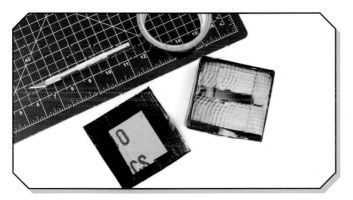

5 Paint your statue. Once the paint dries, use permanent markers to add details. This will make your award really pop.

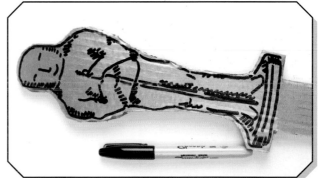

6 Slide your statue's tab into your base's cutout hole. The statue will be a bit wobbly, so cut out a cardboard cross piece to stabilize it.

The statue's tab should fit into the slit.

7 Tape your base onto the slightly larger piece of cardboard.

PROJECT #2

MOVIE CLAPPER

Ready to begin your career in filmmaking? You'll need to mark the beginning and ends of movie scenes. Make yourself a clapper board and start shooting!

SUPPLIES

- scissors
- pencil
- corrugated cardboard
- drill
- tacky glue
- black and white paint
- paintbrush
- metal fastener
- decoupage glue (optional)
- white pencil (optional)
- sponge brush (optional)

Cut out the shapes for your clapper: two identical body parts, two identical large rectangles, and two identical small rectangles.

Small rectangles 1 & 2

Large rectangle 1

Large rectangle 2

Body part 1

Body part 2

Drill holes through the corners of the large rectangles. Then drill holes through the circular bit of the body parts.

 Glue the two body parts to each other, the large rectangles to each other, and the small rectangles to each other. Glue the small rectangles on top of the body. Make sure the holes line up when gluing.

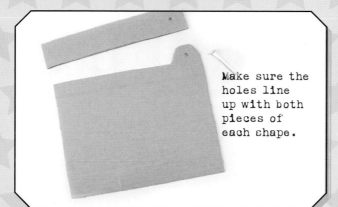

Make sure the holes line up with both pieces of each shape.

 Once the glue dries, paint everything black. Use white paint to add details like the stripes, lines, or words.

TIP
To make the sign shiny and sturdy, cover it with a layer of decoupage glue.

Assemble the clapperboard. Use a fastener to attach the large rectangle on top of the body. Now you're ready to shoot a movie!

MINI TV

Ever think about shooting your own television show or movie? Here's a way to see your dream come true! Make your own cardboard TV and watch your stories come to life!

SUPPLIES

- shoe box
- craft knife
- cutting mat
- ruler
- drill
- metal fasteners
- paper
- markers
- duct tape
- pencil/ chopsticks (taller than the height of your TV/ shoebox)
- scissors
- caps from squeeze pouches, milk jugs, or other
- duct tape
- tape
- Styrofoam block

Cut out a rectangle from your box. This will be your television's screen.

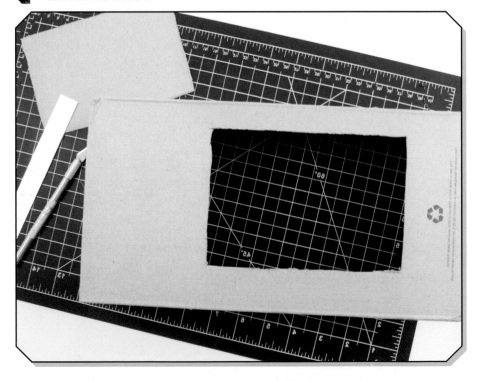

Drill two holes on the top of your television. They should be slightly farther apart than the width of your screen. They should also fit your two pencils.

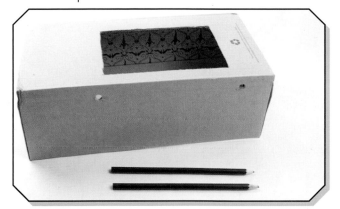

 Drill two holes in the front of your TV. Drill matching holes in two caps. The holes should be big enough to fit your fasteners.

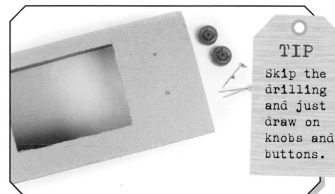

TIP
Skip the drilling and just draw on knobs and buttons.

 Cut out a long sheet of paper to be your storyboard. It's height should be slightly larger than your screen's height. Draw on your story.

TIP
Don't have a long sheet of paper? Tape together several pieces of shorter paper.

 Decorate your television with markers and duct tape. Fasten on your buttons (from step 3).

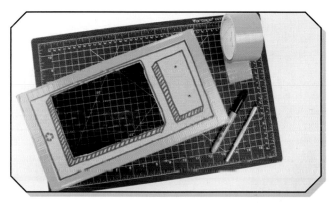

 Place your pencils through the two holes. Tape one end of your story to one pencil. Curl the roll of paper around that pencil. Then tape the other end to the other pencil. Now cut out a piece of Styrofoam. Stick your pencils into the Styrofoam to hold them in place. Tape your Styrofoam down. Now twist the pencil to play your show!

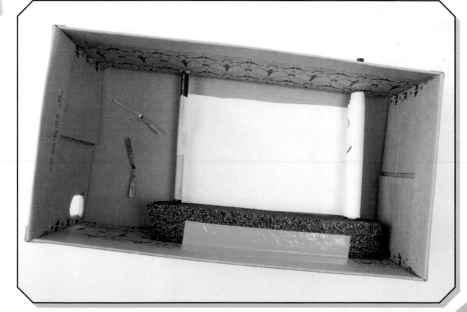

DUCT TAPE BOW TIE

To put on a magic show, you've got to look the part. Whip up these cool and colorful duct tape bow ties to get you on your way!

SUPPLIES

- scissors or craft knife
- cutting mat

- ruler
- duct tape (black, green, gold, yellow, silver)

- hook and loop fastener (optional)

1. Cut a 16-inch (41-cm) strip of duct tape and place it sticky-side up. Fold one third over, then the other third. Use a craft knife or scissors to trim the ends. This will be the strap.

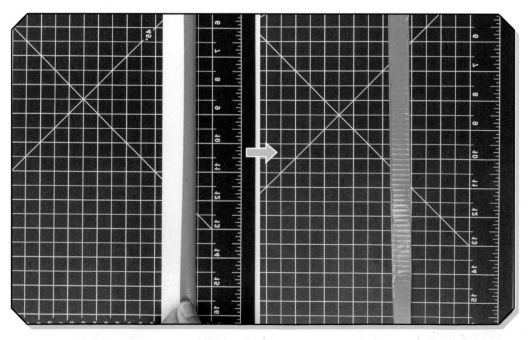

2 Cut two 5-inch (13-cm) pieces of duct tape. This will be for the bow.

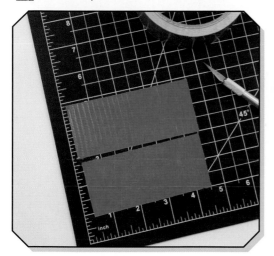

3 Place one on top of the other so that the sticky sides are together. To add a different color trim, wrap both long sides of your duct tape piece with thin strips of different-colored duct tape. Trim off any excess bits.

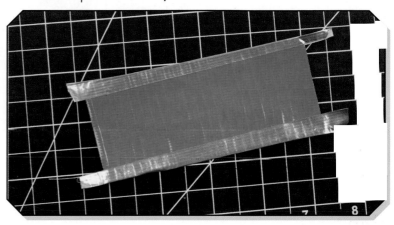

4 Pinch the middle to make a bow shape.

First fold your duct tape strip in half. Then fold both sides in.

5 Use a thin piece of tape to help the bow keep its shape. Then, use a bigger piece of tape to tie the bow onto your strap.

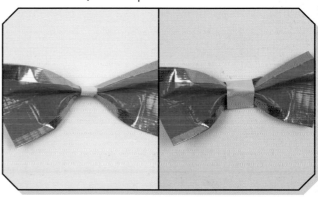

6 Use a thin piece of tape to tape both sides together around your neck.

TIP

Instead of tape, use a hook and loop fastener — then you can wear your bow tie over and over again!

PROJECT #2

MAGIC HAT

Every magician needs a swanky top hat. Where else will you store your rabbits? Make a great hat from cardboard for this awesome craft!

- scissors
- cereal box
- ruler
- stapler

- pencil/marker/pen
- craft knife
- cutting mat
- duct tape

- duct tape
- tacky glue
- black paint
- paintbrush

1 Cut open your cereal box. Cut out a cardboard rectangle big enough to wrap around your head.

TIP
Unsure of your size? Turn to page 52 to learn how to measure your head!

2 Tightly curl your cardboard into a large tube. This will make your hat cylindrical.

3 Make sure your piece of cardboard wraps around your head. If it does, staple it together.

4 Trace your cylinder onto a cereal box.

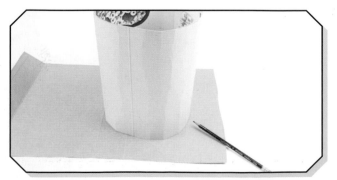

5 Trace a larger circle around your traced circle.

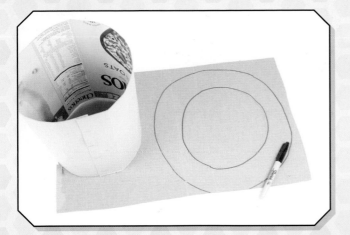

6 Cut out the larger circle and the smaller circle. The smaller circle will be the top of the hat and the larger circle will be the brim.

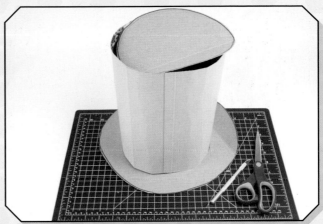

7 To attach the hat to the brim, cut out tabs in the bottom of your cylinder. Slide the cylinder into your brim. Duct tape the tabs to the brim.

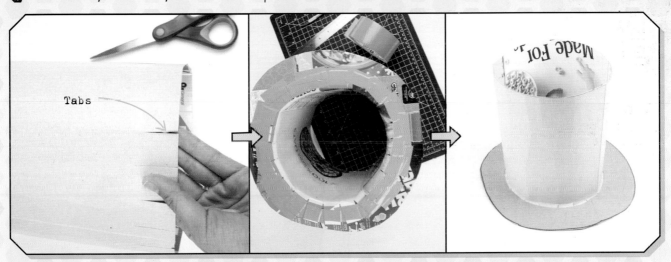

Tabs

8 Attach the top of the hat with tacky glue.

9 Paint the hat and add a strip of duct tape.

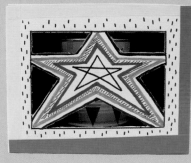

PROJECT #3

MAGIC BOX

Ever dream of having real magic powers? Wouldn't it be cool to make things disappear? Well, with this super rad magic box, you can! Start your magic training here!

- large tin can
- smaller tin can
- cardboard box
- duct tape
- craft knife

- cutting mat
- scissors
- black paint
- paintbrush
- brown paper

- bag (or a thick sheet of paper)
- ruler
- permanent markers

- pencil
- small object (should fit inside the smaller tin can)

1 Make sure that the small tin can fits inside the large tin can, and the large tin can fits inside of your box.

2 Wash and dry your tin cans. Ask an adult to cut off the bottom of the larger tin can.

3 Use duct tape to decorate your larger can.

4 Paint the inside of your box black. Cut out a large rectangular piece of brown paper to wrap around the smaller can. Paint it black.

5 Trim the painted paper so that it fits around your smaller can.

6 Tape the painted paper onto your can with clear tape. Cut out a smaller black rectangle from your remaining painted paper. Tape the smaller sheet inside of your can.

TIP
To fit the can exactly, roll it along the paper and use a pencil to trace the edges of the can while you roll.

7 Create a design for the front of the box with a couple small-sized, cut-out portions. This will allow the audience to glimpse inside. Use a craft knife and cut out portions from the box's front. Decorate the box with permanent markers and duct tape. Make sure to keep the cut-out portions exposed.

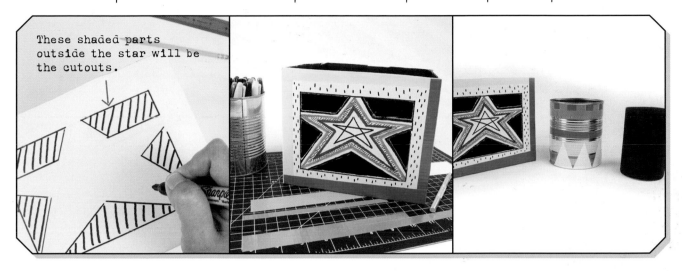

These shaded parts outside the star will be the cutouts.

LET'S MAKE THINGS APPEAR FROM THIN AIR!

BEFORE YOU GATHER YOUR AUDIENCE: Place your colorful can inside of your box. Place your black can inside of your colorful can. Then put a tiny object (toy, scarf, egg, crayon, or whatever) inside of your black can.

BEFORE YOU PERFORM THE TRICK: Place the box on an elevated surface. Seat the audience lower than your box (important!). Tell them that you own a magic box.

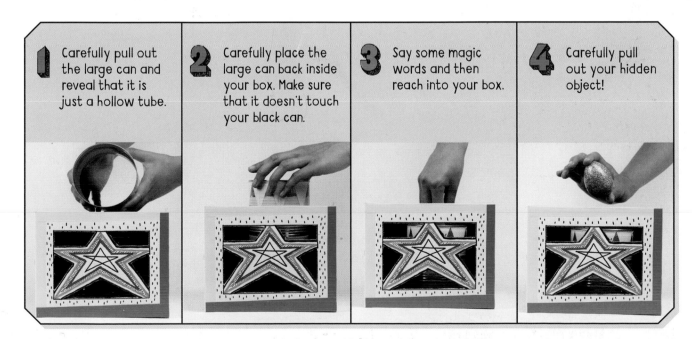

1 Carefully pull out the large can and reveal that it is just a hollow tube.

2 Carefully place the large can back inside your box. Make sure that it doesn't touch your black can.

3 Say some magic words and then reach into your box.

4 Carefully pull out your hidden object!

Race Car Driver

WORK A

Pilot

Firefighter

Secret Agent

COOL JOB

Construction Worker

PROJECT #1

WORKER'S VEST

Ready to build a city? You'll need to make yourself a duct tape construction vest. Bright and reflective, this vest will be sure to keep you safe as you work!

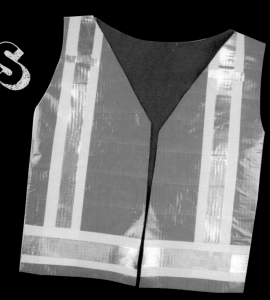

SUPPLIES

- permanent marker
- T-shirt
- cutting mat
- fabric scissors
- duct tape (orange, yellow, and silver)
- craft knife

TIP

Remember, fabric scissors are the best at cutting fabric, but if you don't own a pair, normal scissors will work great too!

Use your marker to sketch out the two front panels and back panel of your vest.

Use your fabric scissors to cut out the two front panels and back panel.

 Cover your fabric panels with strips of duct tape. Make sure to overlap them to fully cover all the fabric. Once you're finished, carefully peel off the fabric and trim off any excess duct tape.

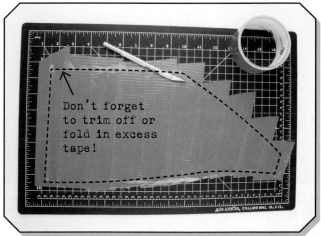

Don't forget to trim off or fold in excess tape!

 Add additional strips of duct tape to add extra details.

 Use strips of duct tape to attach the front panels to the back panel.

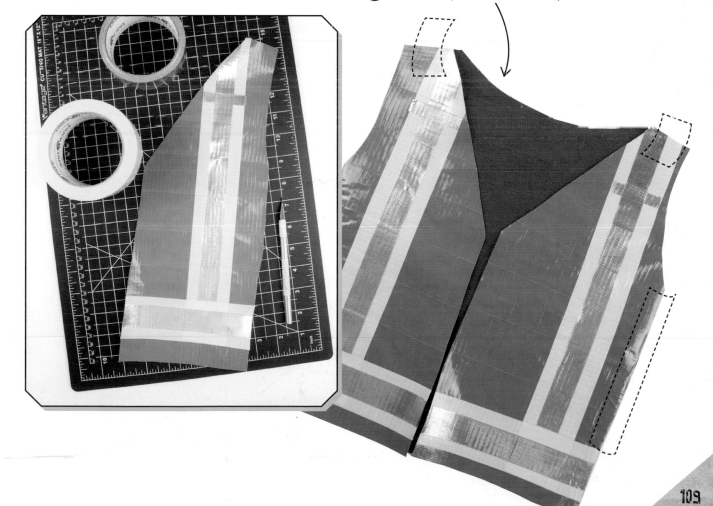

PROJECT #2
CITY

What would your dream home look like? What about your dream neighborhood? Put your imagination to work and design and build your very own cardboard city today!

- corrugated cardboard
- scissors

- permanent markers
- cereal box

- toilet paper rolls
- paint (optional)

3D Buildings:

1 Cut out two identical building shapes. Cut out corresponding stilts in both buildings.

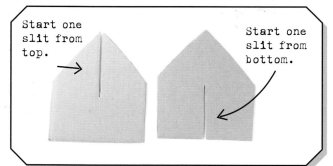

Start one slit from top.

Start one slit from bottom.

2 Add details with permanent markers. Assemble buildings by sliding pieces together.

Puzzle Buildings:

1 Cut out rectangles and squares from cereal box cardboard. Cut out slits in your pieces.

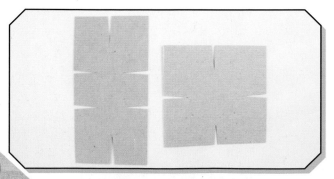

2 Add details with permanent markers. Assemble buildings by sliding pieces together in different configurations.

Tube Buildings:

1 Cut several slits through both ends of your tube.

2 Add details with permanent markers. Assemble by sliding the tubes together.

TIP

As with most of these crafts, if you don't like your design, pull the pieces apart and build again!

Buildings on Stilts:

1 Cut out building shapes. Cut out two tiny tabs for each shape. Also cut out corresponding slits in the pieces.

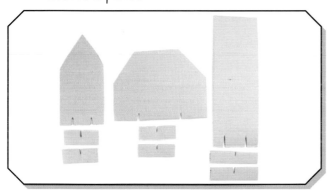

2 Add details with permanent markers. Assemble buildings by sliding pieces together.

The sky's the limit! Add cars, trees, signs, mini figures, or roller coasters! Or, team up! Do this project with a friend to create a large, sprawling city!

111

PROJECT #3
CRANE

It's amazing to watch big construction vehicles do their jobs! With this craft, you can design and operate your own cardboard crane. Put your hard hats on – it's time to get to work!

SUPPLIES

- corrugated cardboard box (we used a pizza box)
- corrugated cardboard
- scissors
- drill
- 2 pipe cleaners
- pencil
- long, narrow box
- paper towel roll
- craft knife
- cutting mat
- smaller box
- glue (hot glue or tacky glue)
- yarn
- plastic container
- permanent markers
- paint
- paintbrush

1 Grab a clean, sturdy box for the base. From a separate piece of cardboard, cut out a circle with a lever.

2 Cut out two same-sized small circles and drill two holes through each of them. Drill one large hole through the centers of your box and your rotating platform.

3 Take a pipe cleaner and bend it through both holes of one small circle. Then string it through the hole in your rotating platform.

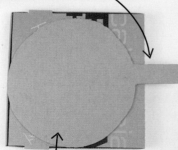

The lever must extend beyond the box's edges.

The circle's size determines the size of your crane.

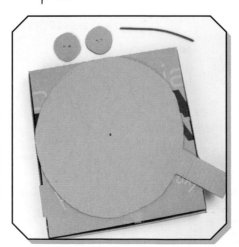

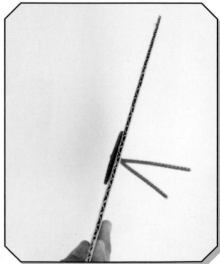

4 String it through the hole in your pizza box. Then, bend it through both holes of your other small circle. Twist the ends together.

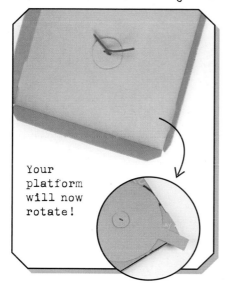

Your platform will now rotate!

 5 Trace a paper towel roll on your tall narrow box.

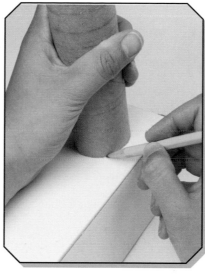

 6 Cut out the circle shape on both opposite sides on the box. You should now have a hole going through your box.

7 Grab a small box and cut out a rectangle from the front. Drill two holes on either side and slide a pencil through.

The pencil should be snug, but you should be able to turn it!

8 Glue on your tower with the hole and your cab with the pencil. Put the paper towel roll through the hole in the tall box.

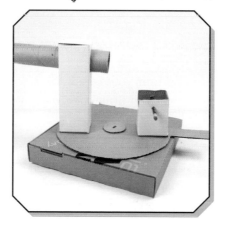

9 Drill two holes in both sides of a small container. Twist pipe cleaner ends through the holes to create a handle.

10 Cut a long piece of yarn. Tie an end to your pencil. Pull your string through the cardboard roll. Tie the dangling end to your container

To raise and lower your container, just turn your pencil.

11 Decorate your crane with markers or paint!

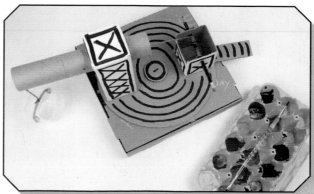

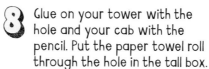

PROJECT #1

GLIDER

Gliders are some of the coolest airplanes out there. Try your hand at designing and flying one of these amazing planes with this cardboard glider craft!

SUPPLIES

•scissors	•cutting mat	•ruler	•clear tape
•cereal box	•pencil	•tape	•markers
•craft knife		•penny	•stickers

1. Cut out three parts from your cereal box: a body, wings, and a horizontal stabilizer. Cut a slit in your glider's body to slip the wings through. Cut a slit in the body and the stabilizer to attach them together.

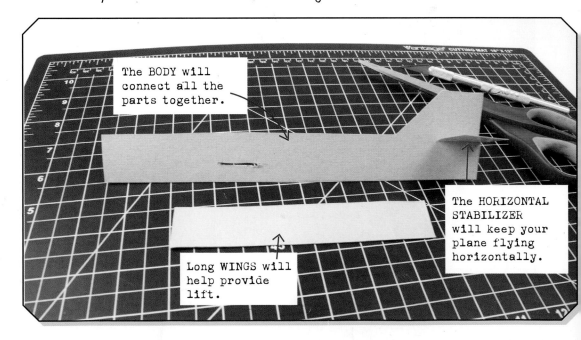

The BODY will connect all the parts together.

The HORIZONTAL STABILIZER will keep your plane flying horizontally.

Long WINGS will help provide lift.

Glider design takes a lot of trial and error. To design the best flying plane, cut out several identical bodies and several wings and horizontal stabilizers of varying lengths. This way you can try out different combinations of wings and stabilizers.

Is your plane not flying well? Time to add other modifications. Tape a weight (like a penny or paper clip) to the front of your plane. This will help the plane fly horizontally. Or fold the wing tips up and see if that helps.

Once you've tested out your own fleet of mix-and-match planes, add more personalized details with markers and stickers.

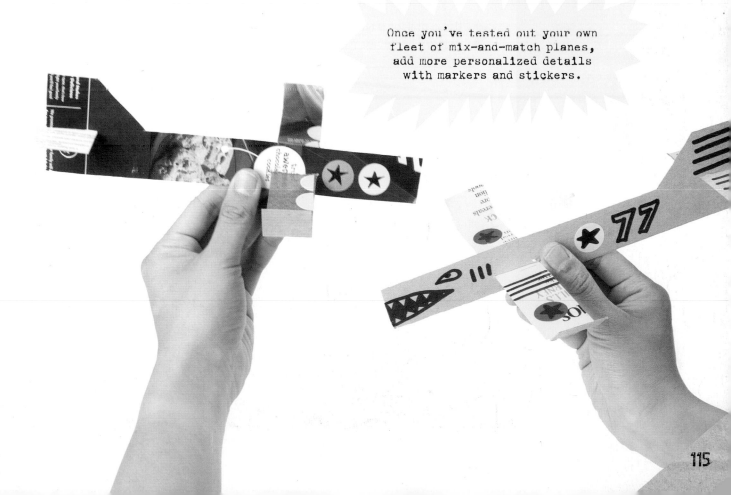

PROJECT #2

AIRPORT WITH LIGHTS!

Have you ever seen an airport runway at night? It's beautiful! Put on your pilot's cap – today we're honing your flying skills with this fun, light-up cardboard airport!

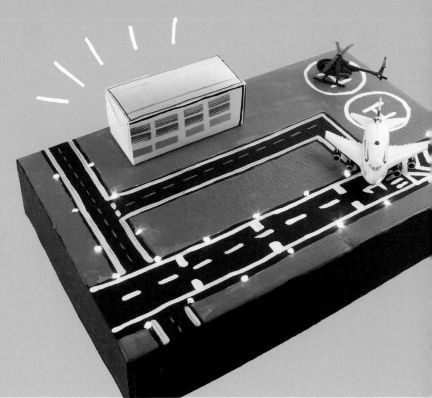

SUPPLIES

- drill (or hammer and nail)
- cardboard box lid
- paint (black, green, yellow, white)
- pencil (white and regular)
- tiny cardboard box
- silver duct tape
- string lights

Use a drill (or a hammer and nail) to pierce the cardboard. This will be where you place your runway lights.

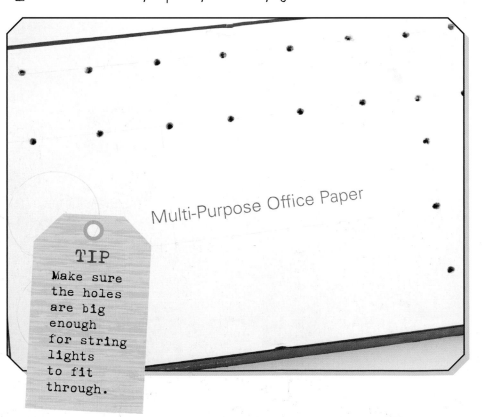

Multi-Purpose Office Paper

TIP
Make sure the holes are big enough for string lights to fit through.

2 Paint your airport. Use real airport images as a guide.

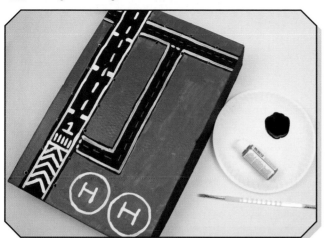

3 Use small boxes as buildings. Decorate them with duct tape and paint. Tape them to the airport.

Silver duct tape does a great job resembling glass!

4 Stick your string lights through the drilled holes. Use duct tape to keep them in place.

TIP
Design your airport runways and landing pads around your airplanes and helicopters.

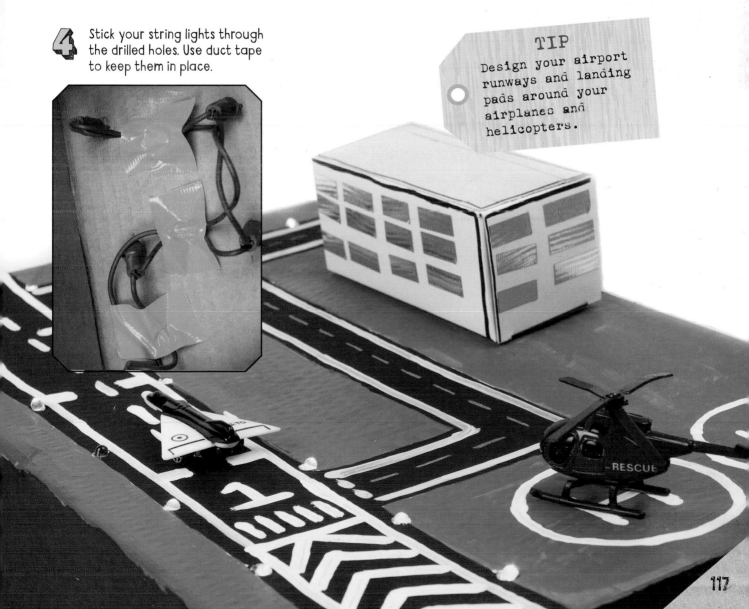

PROJECT #3

COCKPIT

Ever seen the inside of a real cockpit? It's full of instruments that help pilots control aircraft. Start your career as a pilot with your very own cardboard cockpit!

SUPPLIES

- cardboard box with lid
- pencil
- craft knife
- cutting mat

- add-on items: lids, compass, stickers, clothespins, rubber bands, plastic bottles, cardboard pieces, skewer, old keyboard pieces, buttons

- duct tape
- permanent markers
- glue (hot glue or tacky glue)

 Cut out a rectangle in the front of your box.

 Cut out a hole in the middle of your lid to create the windshield.

Collect an assortment of items around your home to be the various instruments and switches on the dashboard.

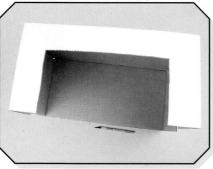

 Decorate your windshield and cockpit with the items.

Doodle on dials or buttons. - - - - -

Use colored duct tape to decorate clothespins.

5 To make the joystick, drill two holes in your box and the bottle lid. Slip the two ends of your rubber band up through the bottom of your box. Now slip the rubber band's two ends through the holes in your lid. Tie a double knot to secure it in place. Screw on your bottle and now you have a moveable bottle joystick!

6 To create your own sliding lever, cut out a slit in your cardboard. Trim a skewer to your desired lever's length. Then cut out two rectangular pieces of corrugated cardboard. Each piece should be approximately half the length of your skewer. Use tacky glue to lightly coat the ends of your skewer. Push the skewer through the slit and cap both ends with corrugated cardboard. The skewer should fit inside the holes in the cardboard.

The slit should be wide enough to just fit a skewer.

The skewer is wedged within these rectangular pieces

7 Glue or tape your windshield onto your base. You're all set to take flight!

TIP

Make the hole from step 1 large enough for your legs to fit under the box. Then, cut out another similarly sized hole in the back of your box. Now you can sit underneath the cockpit!

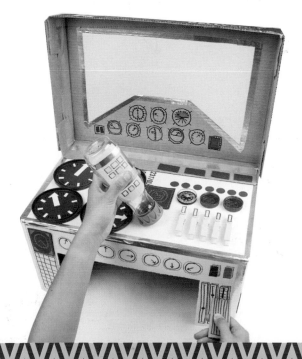

SECRET AGENT

PROJECT #1
CIPHER

As a secret agent, you'll need a way to pass messages to others. But how can you keep them secret? Make these cool ciphers to get the information in the right hands!

SUPPLIES

- cereal box
- scissors
- pencil
- drill (or hammer and nail)
- 4 metal fasteners
- markers

1 Cut out four large identical circles. Cut out four small identical circles. Drill a hole in the middle of each circle.

2 Pair each small circle with a large circle. Use a fastener to attach them together.

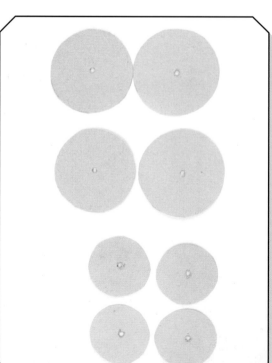

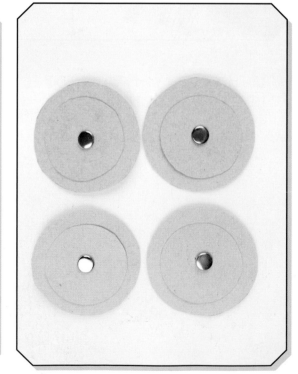

120

3 Draw lines through the circles to create eight equal segments. Label the inside segments with numbers and the outside segments with letters.

LABELING GUIDE

A–H with 1–8	Q–X with 17–24
I–P with 9–16	Y–Z with 25–32

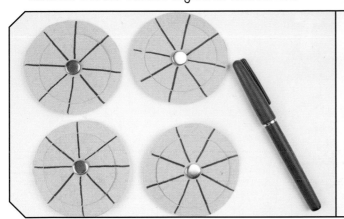 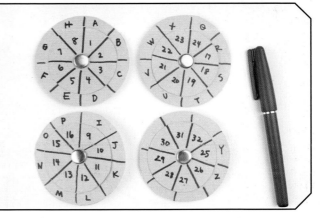

 4 **To create different types of codes:**

Use markers to make a pair of matching shapes on one letter and one number on each circle. Do this with one color marker to make one code, or with a few colored markers to make more codes.

To write out a coded message:

Turn the circles so the shapes of a certain color match. In the example below, the pink shapes are aligned. Then write out your message in pink using the numbers for each letter you want to use.

To decode the message:

Your recipient needs to first figure out which color shapes to align. The pen color you used to write the message is her clue. So she should line up the pink colors and shapes and plug in the corresponding letters under your numerical message!

CRACK THE CODE!

Ready for your first mission? Test your spy moves by cracking the code below! (Answer is on the side.)

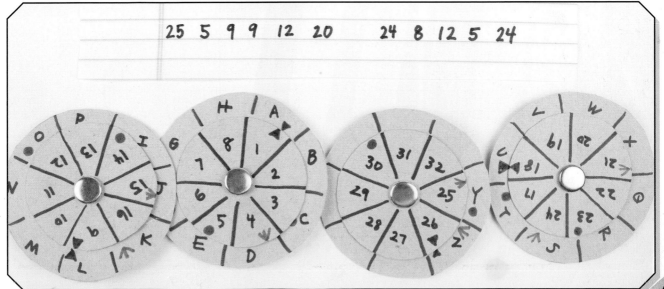

25 5 9 9 12 20   24 8 12 5 24

Answer: YELLOW SHOES

PROJECT #2
UTILITY BELT

As a secret agent, you need lots of secret pockets. Make this cool utility belt to hold all your spy gadgets and gear!

SUPPLIES

- craft knife
- cutting mat
- duct tape
- clear tape
- scissors
- permanent marker

(To make the duct tape belt)
Cut out two identical pieces of duct tape. Flip one so that it's sticky-side up. Place the other piece of duct tape on top to make a two-sided strap.

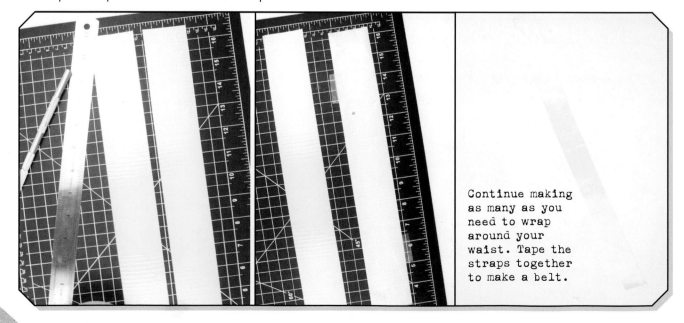

Continue making as many as you need to wrap around your waist. Tape the straps together to make a belt.

2 (To make narrow pockets)

Cut out two identical strips of duct tape. Flip one piece so that it's sticky-side up. Place one piece of duct tape on top of the other. Fold the bottom of the strip partially up. Tape both sides together with duct tape. Use scissors to trim the flap.

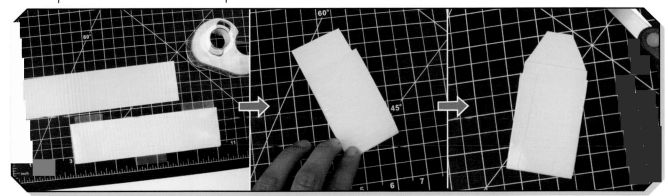

3 (To make wider pockets)

Instead of using one strip, you'll use two overlapping pieces of duct tape to create the pocket. Follow the same steps above to finish the pocket.

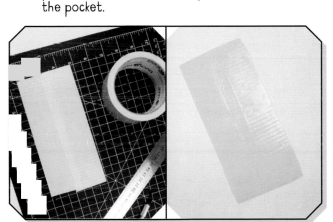

4 Use duct tape to tape the pockets to your belt.

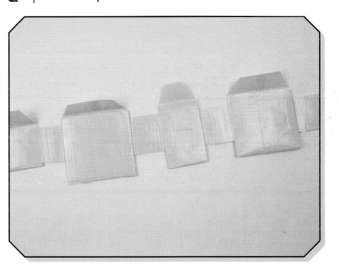

5 Use permanent markers to add extra details. Then get to spying!

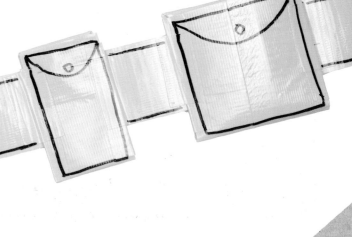

NOTE BOOK

Imagine you're watching and taking notes on a target when he spots you. Surprised, he asks to see your notebook. You casually flip through and show him drawings and doodles. He leaves, and you relax. Now you flip through the notebook and reveal secret notes. How is this possible? It's your secret magic notebook. Flip it one way and you see what you want people to see. Flip it another way and you reveal your secret notes. Spy materials don't get cooler than this!

SUPPLIES

- cereal box
- scissors
- craft knife
- cutting mat
- markers
- pencil
- white paper
- stapler

1 Cut out a long rectangle to make the notebook's cover.

2 Fold this in half.

Use a craft knife and cut out two holes from the front of your notebook. Then use markers to decorate the front and back covers.

You can peek through these holes while pretending to "read" your notebook!

 Make the inside of your notebook! Trace your notebook cover onto sheets of white paper.

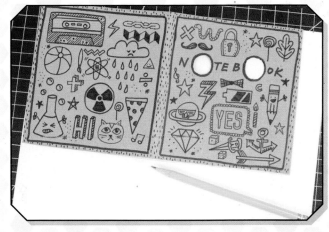

Cut the sheets out.

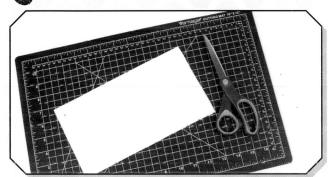

Cut those sheets of paper in half.

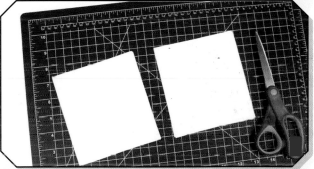

Here's the secret step to making our magic notebook! Split your cut sheets into two equal piles of paper. Then cut one side of each pile of papers on a slant. Now one pile of papers will have a longer top and shorter bottom. The other pile of papers will have a shorter top and a longer bottom.

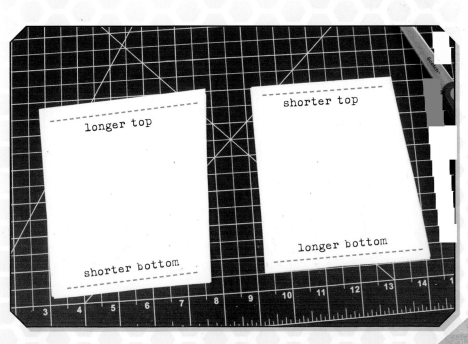

longer top

shorter bottom

shorter top

longer bottom

8 Put the two pile of papers together in an alternating fashion. So you will end up with a pile of papers that look something like this - one top long sheet, one bottom long sheet, one top long sheet, one bottom long sheet, etc...

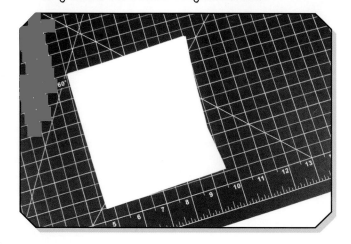

9 Place your pile of sheets inside your notebook cover. Staple the book together.

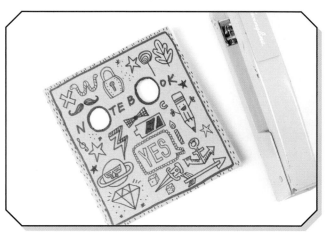

HOW TO USE YOUR MAGIC SPY NOTEBOOK:

HOW TO USE THE SPY HOLES

Simply open up your notebook to the first page. Peer out the holes at other people without them realizing!

Every odd page (1st, 3rd, 5th, 7th, etc) should all be the same - either all top long or all bottom long. Draw or write the messages that you WANT people to see on these pages.

Every even page (2nd, 4th, 6th, etc) will be your spy note pages. Write secret notes on these pages that you don't want other people seeing.

Odd Pages (For all to see)

Even Pages (For spy eyes only)

HOW TO REVEAL ONLY NON-SECRET MESSAGES OR ONLY SECRET MESSAGES TO OTHERS

When you flip through your pages, you can either place your right thumb on the top of your notebook, or on the bottom of the notebook.

To reveal non-secret messages:

Look at your first page. See if it's a top long page or bottom long page. If it's a top long page, flip your notebook with your thumb on the top. If it's a bottom long page, flip your notebook with your thumb on the bottom.

My notebook starts with a top long page. My thumb is on the top. When I flip the pages, I show people doodles.

To reveal secret messages:

See if your even pages are top long pages or bottom long pages. If it's a top long page, flip your notebook with your thumb on the top. If it's a bottom long page, flip your notebook with your thumb on the bottom.

My secret messages are on bottom long pages. So, my thumb is on the bottom. When I flip the pages, I now reveal my secret spy notes.

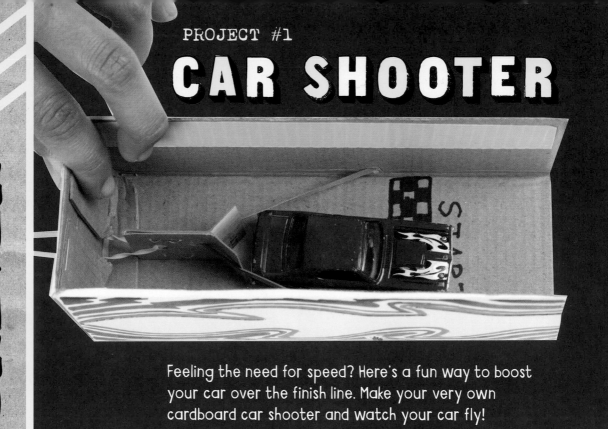

CAR SHOOTER

Feeling the need for speed? Here's a fun way to boost your car over the finish line. Make your very own cardboard car shooter and watch your car fly!

SUPPLIES

- narrow cardboard box
- scissors
- cutting mat
- stapler
- duct tape
- drill (or hammer and nail)
- toy cars
- cereal box cardboard
- pen
- hole punch
- stapler
- 2 rubber bands
- permanent markers

1 Cut off the top and side of a narrow cardboard box.

2 Reinforce the remaining side with staples and duct tape. This will be the back of your shooter.

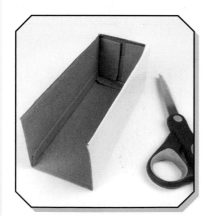

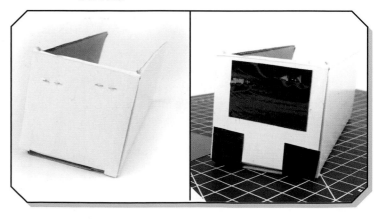

Drill two holes in the back of your shooter.

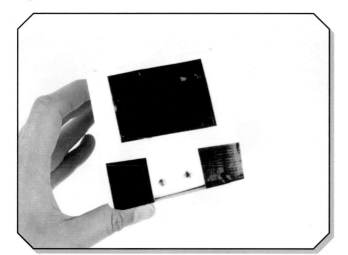

 Drill two holes in each side of your shooter. These holes should be at least 1 ½ car lengths away from the back of your shooter, so your rubber band will have room to be pulled back. The holes should be parallel to each other.

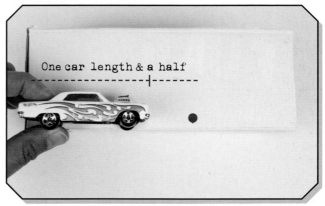

One car length & a half

 Cut out a small cardboard rectangle. Fold it in half.

 Punch two holes in it. Staple the piece together. Bend out the top portion to create two tabs.

Cut two rubber bands loops. String one through the holes in the side of your shooter and one of the holes in your cardboard rectangle. Tie both ends together underneath your shooter.

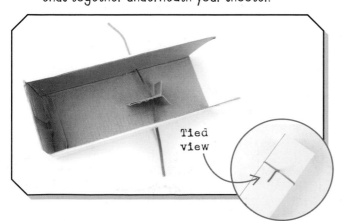

Tied view

String the other rubber band through the back two holes of your shooter and the back hole of your folded cardboard rectangle. Tie both ends together. Now grab your car and make it fly!

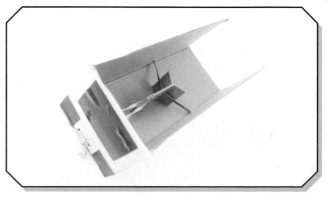

PROJECT #2
RACING FLAG

Ready to speed across the finish line? Celebrate your winning car's victory with his checkered duct tape racing flag!

- craft knife
- cutting mat

- duct tape (black, yellow, and white)

- garbage bag
- scissors

- wooden dowel

1 Use your craft knife and cut four equal strips of duct tape. Place them next to each other on your cutting mat. (They should not be touching.)

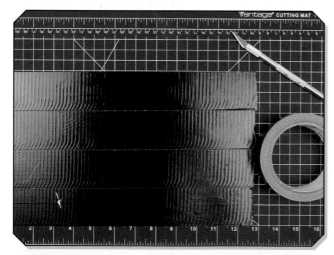

2 Lift up two pieces of black duct tape. Place a piece of white duct tape over the remaining two strips.

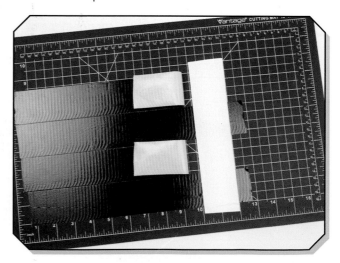

Place your lifted pieces of duct tape down. Now lift up the other two piece of duct tape from the other side. Place a piece of white duct tape over the remaining pieces of black duct tape.

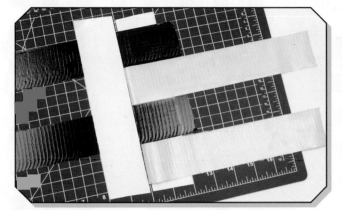

 Continue this pattern of lifting and taping to weave the black and white checkerboard pattern. Once you're done, carefully pull it off the cutting mat.

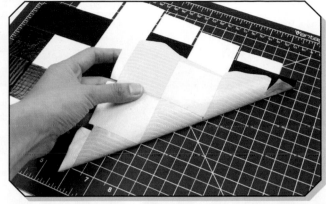

 Flip it over and place a piece of garbage bag over the sticky side. Smooth everything out and trim the bag to create a black and white rectangle.

 Repeat steps 1–5 to create another checkerboard design. Place your first woven flag over this new woven flag. Trim the edges with a craft knife.

 Add some decorative yellow trim and tape the two pieces together.

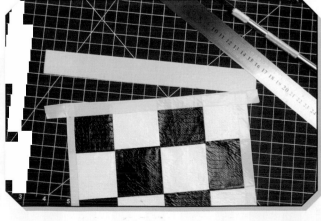

 Adhere your flag to your wooden dowel with another piece of duct tape.

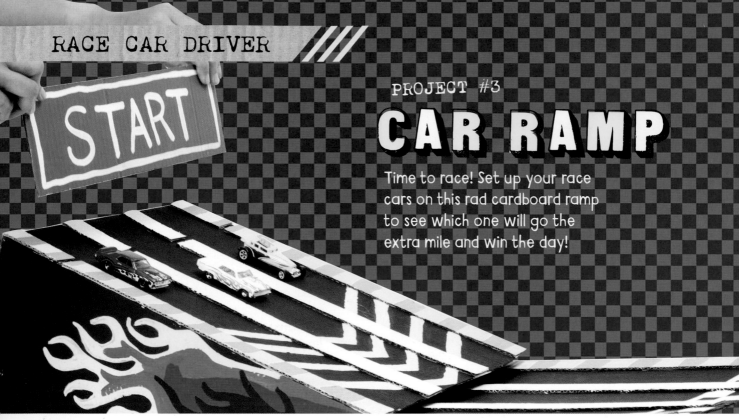

CAR RAMP

Time to race! Set up your race cars on this rad cardboard ramp to see which one will go the extra mile and win the day!

SUPPLIES

- medium/large sized box
- pencil
- corrugated cardboard
- scissors
- ruler
- tacky glue
- paint
- paintbrush
- permanent markers
- white pencil

1 Draw a diagonal line across one side of your box. Cut it out.

2 Cut out another side and another triangle from your cardboard box. Now you should be left with a box that looks like a wedge of cheese.

TIP

Notice where the bottom of your box is. Make sure you keep the bottom of the box connected and in tact! That will be your ramp.

To lengthen your ramp, cut out a cardboard rectangle that has the same width as your ramp.

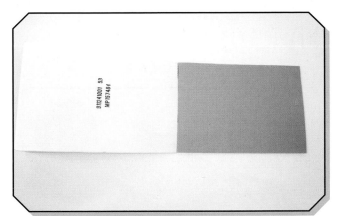

 Cut out a rectangle to be your "start" board. This will ensure that all the race cars start at the same time. It's length should be the same as your ramp's width. This way your rubber band will have room to be pulled back.

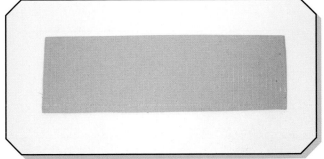

5 Cut out cardboard strips to act as the lane markers and the side rails of your ramp and cardboard straightaway. The strips should all be the same width. Their lengths should match the ramp and straightaway's lengths.

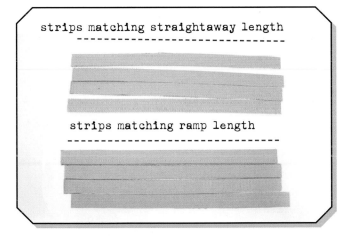

strips matching straightaway length

strips matching ramp length

6 We're going to make sure the "start" board fits into the ramp strips. Cut your strip one car's length away from an end. Make this same cut for all your ramp strips.

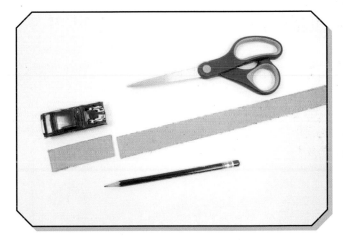

7 Glue your straightaway strips to the straightaway.

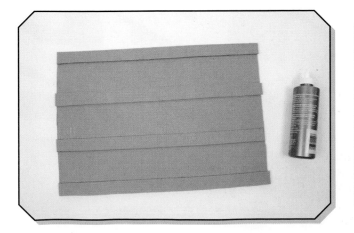

 Glue your ramp pieces to the ramp. Make sure you leave a space for your "start" board on the ramp!

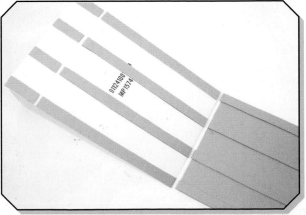

9 Check to make sure your start board fits in the slots on the ramp.

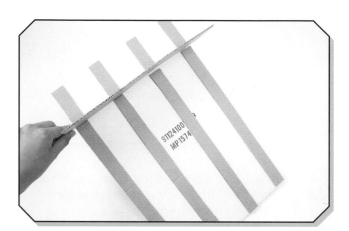

10 Paint your ramp, straightaway piece, and start board.

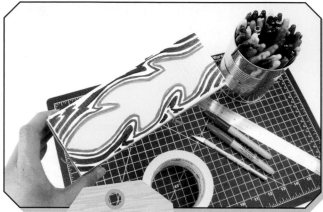

TIP
If your piece is painted black, use a white pencil to draw in lines.

11 Once your paint dries, set up your race car ramp by placing your ramp on top of your straightaway piece. Then slide your "start" board in place and put your cars in their lanes.

YOU'RE ALL SET TO RACE!

FIRE JACKET

Ready to save some lives? Make this firefighter jacket and be a part of the team that puts out fires and saves homes, people, and pets! Who needs a cape? With this jacket, you're a real hero!

FIREFIGHTER

SUPPLIES

- black T-shirt
- yellow and silver duct tape
- ruler
- fabric scissors

Decorate the shirt with strips of yellow and silver duct tape.

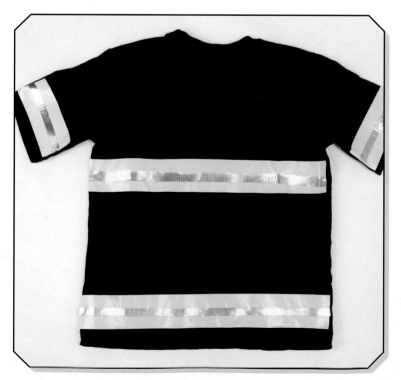

Cut the front of the shirt in half.

TIP
Use a pair of fabric scissors to make the neatest cut. If you don't own a pair, normal scissors will do.

3 Add extra details (like buckles) with duct tape.

PROJECT #2
FIRES

Firefighters have to do a lot of training. Start your training today with these cardboard fires. Once they're finished, practice putting them out! Have fun, hero!

SUPPLIES

- scissors
- paper
- pencil
- corrugated cardboard
- red, orange, yellow, gold paint
- paintbrush

Cut out a template for a fire. Then trace it two times onto a piece of cardboard. Cut the pieces out.

For each pair of flames, cut out one slit on the top and one slit on the bottom.

 Slide the two pieces together to create a flame. Then paint them.

 Make several big fires and small fires and start putting them out. Your training starts now!

PROJECT #3
HOSE

To put out a fire, you have to have the right tools! Make a handy hose from cardboard to help you beat the fire and save the day!

SUPPLIES

- 2 toilet roll tubes
- scissors
- stapler
- masking tape
- duct tape
- craft mat
- craft knife
- hole punch
- ruler
- 2 rubber bands
- pom-poms (or marshmallows)

1 Each "hose" is made up of two toilet roll tubes. One is normal sized and the other is smaller in diameter so that it fits inside the normal sized tube.

2 Use masking tape to cover one end of the smaller tube.

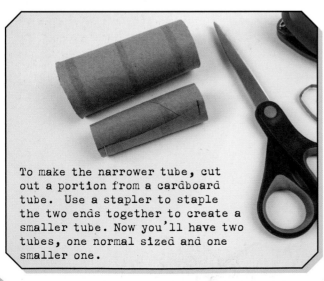

To make the narrower tube, cut out a portion from a cardboard tube. Use a stapler to staple the two ends together to create a smaller tube. Now you'll have two tubes, one normal sized and one smaller one.

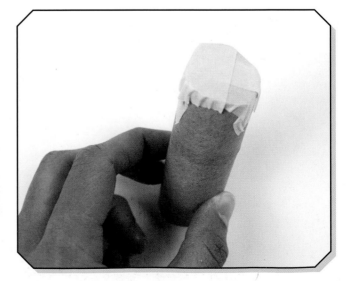

3 Decorate both tubes with duct tape.

 4 Hole punch two holes on the opposite sides of each other in both tubes.

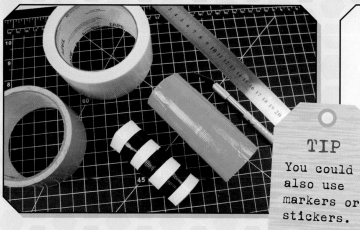

TIP
You could also use markers or stickers.

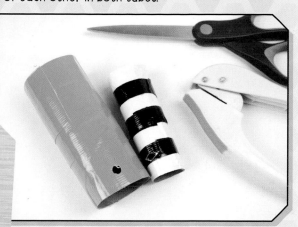

 5 Grab your two rubber bands. Tie each one through a hole in the larger tube.

 6 Thread the ends of the rubber band through the holes in your smaller tube.

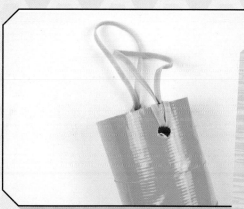

TIP
If your hole puncher will not punch the cardboard, use scissors to cut out openings.

 7 Tie the two rubber bands together. You've now got your pulling device. Your hose is set!

To shoot pom-poms, simply drop a pom-pom in your hose's opening. Pull back the rubber band knot. Aim and let go. Your pom-pom should sail across the room.

ABOUT THE AUTHOR

Leslie Manlapig

Leslie is a full-time mom and sometimes puppeteer who adores books, donuts, and the color yellow. She's always on the lookout for new ways to play and make things with kids. You can read about her family's creative and crafty adventures on her blog www.PinkStripeySocks.com.

FURTHER RESOURCES

NOT GREAT AT FREE-HAND DRAWING?

We've got you covered!
Download templates for many
of the crafts in this book. Visit

www.capstonepub.com/
dabblelabresources

Epic Cardboard Adventures is published by
Capstone Young Readers
1710 Roe Crest Drive
North Mankato, Minnesota 56003
www.mycapstone.com

Library of Congress Cataloging-in-Publication data is
available on the Library of Congress website.

ISBN: 978-1-62370-931-0

Summary: The creator behind the blog, Pink Stripey
Socks, brings her crafting talent to cardboard! With
these easy-to-make, imagination-growing cardboard
crafts, kids can put on a show, travel back in time, and
even rocket to outer space!

Designer: Aruna Rangarajan
Media Researcher: Tracy Cummins
Production Specialist: Tori Abraham

Image credits: All photos by Leslie Manlapig and
Enrico Manlapig, except the following:
Shutterstock: abeadev, Design Element, Boyan
Dimitrov, 15 (tape strips), Coprid, 15 (yarn), DSBfoto,
15 (velcro), Jakub Krechowicz, Front Cover (cardboard
background), Design Element, KannaA, Design Element,
Kiselev Andrey Valerevich, Design Element, kostudio,
12 (boy), KsanaGraphica, Design Element, maxim
ibragimov, 126 (child), Patrick Foto, Cover (girl),
22 (girl), Picsfive, Design Element, Raksha Shelare,
24 (boy), Sylwia Brataniec, 15 (rope), Winai Tepsuttinun,
Back Cover (box), Design Element

Printed in China.
010736S18